ELIZABETH I

and the

Unity of England

ELIZABETH I

and the

Unity of England

by

JOEL HURSTFIELD

Perennial Library
Harper & Row, Publishers, New York

TO
JENNIFER AND JULIAN

Contents

Preface

I HAVE WRITTEN here a political biography of Elizabeth I. This is not because I regard the personal side as unimportant; quite the reverse. Many instances will be found in the following pages where the queen's changing mood and personal intervention affected the development of events at a decisive moment in history.

But I have tried also to show that the governing ideal of her long rule was the restoration and preservation of English unity; an ideal for which she had to fight, sometimes even against the opposition of her ablest subjects. Why she sought it, what barriers she overcame, how she made her rule effective and lasting, and what happened to the Elizabethan system in her closing years, are some of the questions I have tried to answer in this book. In the process I have considered how these issues were reflected in the economy, literature and society of the age.

I am much indebted to Dr A. L. Rowse, the general editor, and to Dr John Scarisbrick, of Queen Mary College, for their comments, and, once again, to Mrs Audrey Munro for typing my manuscript.

UNIVERSITY COLLEGE,   J. H.
LONDON
October, 1959

Chapter One

The Years of Confusion, 1533–58

IN the early days of September 1533, Queen Anne Boleyn, the second wife of Henry VIII, waited at Greenwich for the birth of her child. It was her first and, as is often the case, she hoped for a son. Whatever private emotions provoked this desire, they were quickened and made urgent by overriding political considerations. For Henry Tudor was now in his forty-third year, and still without a male heir. Had she given birth to a son, he would have saved her from the execution block to which she was to be hurried less than three years later, as the king impatiently prepared for his third marriage. These developments she could hardly have foreseen, though chilling fears may have occasionally broken into her thoughts during those idle September days at the king's riverside palace on the Thames.

In due course she was delivered of a fine daughter who, as it turned out, inaugurated the first scene of the personal tragedy of Anne Boleyn. But the occasion was far more important than that. For the birth of Elizabeth Tudor on September 7, 1533 was the living symbol that the unity of England was broken, probably for ever.

Long before, Henry's relations with his first wife,

Katharine of Aragon, had grown cheerless and sterile, and he had found ways of satisfying his passions elsewhere. One such union had produced a son, Henry Fitzroy, Duke of Richmond, upon whom he lavished affection, titles and office; but the bar sinister stood between Richmond and the crown. From time to time Henry had toyed with the idea of inserting his son, by one means or another, into the legitimate line of succession. But he had rightly judged that he dared not stake his dynasty on a gamble. The Wars of the Roses were too recent for that. To bring Richmond in would be to bequeath to faction the bloody prospects of a disputed succession.

But supposing that, after his death, men fell to disputing the title of his legal heir, Mary, sole surviving child of his marriage to Katharine of Aragon? They could not—at present—challenge her legitimacy; but they might make her womanhood a bar to the succession. If they did, they could call upon no English law to support them. But they could call upon history as an ally. Four centuries earlier a woman, Matilda, had claimed the succession; but the struggle against her had grown bitter and memorable during the 'nineteen long winters' of war and confusion. Henry may have wondered whether Englishmen would acquiesce more readily in the succession of Mary than their ancestors had done in the succession of Matilda. The only safeguard against the threat of civil war would be an heir who was both masculine and legitimate. So perforce he began his double quest for a nullification of his marriage to Katharine and for her substitute in both his heart and the state. It was marvellous to behold the way passion and policy kept in step.

In bestowing his affections upon Anne, Henry was not making his first amorous advances to the Boleyn family. Her elder sister Mary had been the king's mistress. But her role had been personal and transient rather than political; and soon she was married. Now it was different. For if Anne had a native liveliness as well as a touch of the Gallic gaiety and wit she had acquired at the French court, she was also driven by a cold ambition which would refuse a king's bed if it did not bring with it a queen's throne. Established as a lady-in-waiting to Katharine of Aragon, Anne had probably by the late 1520s caught her first glimpse of the distant prize, if only she could control a warm heart with a wise head. Control it she did. 'My Lady Anne,' said Katharine to her, at a game of cards, while relations were still formally polite, ' . . . you will have all or none.' It was a sharp assessment. At some stage Anne made it clear to the king that it was all—or nothing at all.

From now onwards Henry, with the help of his minister, Cardinal Wolsey, was engaged in extracting himself from a marriage whose emotional bonds—if they ever existed at all—had long since withered and died. Unfortunately its political bonds seemed to tighten as the queen's nephew, the Emperor Charles V, advanced to a dominant position over Rome. For it was from here alone that annulment of the marriage could come. But the pope was now powerless to grant it, even had he wished to. So there followed a long and complex series of negotiations in which the papal representative, Cardinal Campeggio, established beyond doubt that diplomatic genius consisted in an infinite capacity for wasting time. For as long as possible Henry tried for a compromise; tried to gain from the pope self-determination—not in religion—but in marriage. But at last he came to believe that the only way to break the bonds with Katharine was to break the bonds with Rome.

At which stage he accepted the logic of events we do not know: probably much later than used to be thought. Perhaps towards the end of 1532, with the death of old Archbishop Warham and the emergence of Cranmer, a far more flexible pilot in the troubled waters of ecclesiastical affairs, Henry saw a way to a solution. Perhaps the rising star of Thomas Cromwell lit up a new prospect for the king. Whatever the explanation, it seems that by January 1533, or perhaps a little earlier, Henry was able to assure Anne that, if she yielded now, she would one day be Queen of England. At the same time he must have been able to assure himself that the offspring of the union would be legitimate and in the direct line of the succession. Nine months later Elizabeth Tudor was born: seven and a half months after Henry had been secretly married to Anne Boleyn and less than five months after his marriage to Katharine had been declared null by Thomas Cranmer, now Archbishop of Canterbury.

Henry always remembered his debt to his new Archbishop. To Cranmer alone, of all his ministers, he maintained throughout his life some degree of loyalty.

But the birth of Elizabeth did not solve Henry's problems; it aggravated them. The annulment of his marriage to Katharine had *ipso facto* illegitimatized Mary. As a result Henry now had to face the fact that he no longer had, as heir to the throne, a woman of seventeen, for she had been translated by a stroke of the pen into an illegitimate claimant. In her place was not a son but a baby girl, herself illegitimate in the eyes of half Europe, and of half the king's own subjects as well. Instead of one certain heir he had now presented England with the dread prospect of a succession disputed over by two tainted female claimants. It looked as though he had made certain the very thing he had striven to avoid. 'God', wrote the imperial ambassador in London to his master, Charles V, 'has entirely abandoned this king.' It was something of an understatement.

Time might yet bring a male heir to Henry and Anne, in which case all his efforts would be justified. But time was the essence of the contract. Henry could not wait indefinitely; and, by 1536, the marriage had brought, apart from Elizabeth, only the bitter fruit of a miscarried child. Meanwhile the disillusioned Henry had begun to turn his attention elsewhere. So his second wife had to go the way of his first.

But the succession—and indeed the security of the state—was bound up inextricably with the legality of his marriages. Accordingly, Henry had to call into action the whole apparatus of a state trial in order to release him from wedlock, so that he could *legally* marry again. Anne was accused—and found guilty— of unspeakable crimes, for which she was in due course executed. Whether the trial reached a just verdict, or whether the whole thing was a travesty from start to finish, we shall probably never know. Reasons of state no less than emotion hastened the king along the course he was taking. Soon he was a free man again.

The impartial hand of death struck three times in the same year at the family of Henry VIII. In January 1536 it fell upon Katharine of Aragon, his first consort. In May upon Anne Boleyn, his second, this time at the behest of the king. In July death took off his only son, the Duke of Richmond. In the summer of 1536 Elizabeth Tudor, like her half-sister, Mary, found herself motherless and illegitimate. Mary Tudor was 20 years of age—Elizabeth was not yet three.

In the twilight uncertainty between damnation and a throne, Elizabeth Tudor grew from childhood into adolescence and from adolescence into womanhood. Yet if her position was obscure and dangerous, it was, while her father lived, neither unhappy nor uncomfortable. For she had lost none of the splendours of royalty and her household was that of a Tudor princess, the daughter of King Harry. Towards the end of the reign, her mother's sin—if sin there was—had been virtually blotted out. Elizabeth was installed in the state apartments of Whitehall Palace—and later at Hatfield and

Enfield—and restored also in the direct line of the succession.

Meanwhile she maintained a warm intimate friendship with her young half-brother Edward (born to Jane Seymour, Henry's third wife); and when, in 1547, he succeeded his father as Edward VI, they kept up a happy and—so far as was practicable—informal contact. With Mary, too, Elizabeth remained on good, though less familiar, terms. But Mary was old enough to be her mother; and, in any case, fundamental differences of temperament and religion divided them. Still, there was a basic loyalty between them and, in the dark days which sometimes overtook them, each experienced something of what the other must have endured. The rise of Elizabeth's mother had destroyed the last hopes of Mary's mother, Katharine. The rise of Edward's mother had sped Elizabeth's mother to the block. Yet these events, apparently, did nothing to embitter the relations between the three children. The second generation bore no grudge.

Amid rapidly changing social and political scenes Elizabeth's education proceeded; and it was the best that the age had to offer. Among those who taught her were two such scholars as John Cheke, her brother's tutor, and Roger Ascham—who was one day to write *The Scholemaster*, a celebrated textbook on the theory and practice of education. Of French, Italian and Latin she acquired a good working knowledge; and she was guided by Ascham through some of the classical authors as well as through St Cyprian, one of the

Christian Fathers, whose lucubrations in Latin on 'The Discipline of Virgins' must have tested the endurance of this lively daughter of Henry VIII.

Ascham thought highly of her as a pupil: he considered that she shone like a bright star even in the small galaxy of educated women of the time. He taught her much including, he believed, the appreciation of a literary style 'chaste in its propriety and beautiful by perspicuity'; but the virtues of simplicity she never wholly learned. She could indeed speak with a vivid candour—and, on occasion, with an earthly frankness more appropriate to a warlike king than a virgin queen. But some of her speeches are marked by a flamboyant obscurity which bewildered her contemporaries as much as they have baffled her historians. Part, at least, of the obscurity must have been deliberate. For Elizabeth had other teachers to instruct her, apart from Roger Ascham.

Her greatest teacher, undoubtedly, was experience. In the political jungle of the mid-Tudor period she was submitted to a course of instruction as harsh as it was subtle. It taught her that she must bury her emotions beyond the reach of the politicians. She proved an apt pupil; and not a moment too soon. For she was shortly the object, though not the author, of one of many plots.

It is well known that, in the eighteenth century, practising politicians organized their manoeuvres with a wary eye upon the heir to the throne. The same was true in the second half of the sixteenth century. In 1547 Edward was on the throne; but he was a child and a considerable way from marriage. If he died childless then Mary would succeed. But if he died within a few years of coming to the throne, so might Mary, as indeed she did. In that event Elizabeth would succeed as the last of her line; and upon her marriage would hinge the whole dynasty—and perhaps the unity and the destiny of England as well. Here was a marriage prospect as attractive as it was dangerous; and to Elizabeth it brought a brief and scandalous wooing. It entangled her also, for a while, in a web of high political intrigue.

Soon after the accession of Edward VI, one of his uncles was installed as Lord Protector Somerset. Another uncle was the Lord Admiral, Thomas Seymour, less public spirited, more vainglorious than his brother. After considering various ladies for his bride, the admiral divided his attentions between Katharine Parr, the queen-dowager, and Elizabeth her stepdaughter; but he made his first bid for Elizabeth. She was then fourteen years of age, and she refused him with the tactful plea of her extreme youth. So Seymour married Katharine—four or five months after the death of her late husband, Henry VIII. But marriage did not immunize him to the charms of Elizabeth, living at that time in her stepmother's household; and he proceeded to make use of the opportunities at hand. 'Nothing but the coarse romping of the times' is the way in which one Victorian historian describes the incidents; and he was probably right. But Seymour's cheap and intimate gallantries with a young girl on the threshold of woman-

hood discredit him as a man as much as they disqualify
him as a statesman. At last, even the good-tempered
Katharine was affronted; and prudence—or pressure
—caused Elizabeth to withdraw. But within a year
Katharine had died in childbed, and Seymour was free
to start again. He did so without delay.

This was too much for the Lord Protector. A clandestine marriage between Elizabeth and the admiral
would strengthen faction and threaten the already
weakening grasp of the Protector on the reins of government. Under pressure from the Council he acted
swiftly. He clapped his brother in the Tower and
charged him with high treason, including 'his purpose
of marrying the said Lady Elizabeth, to the danger of
the King's Majesty's person, and peril of the state of
the same'. Elizabeth herself had to submit to close
questioning. In answer she generously supplied a great
mass of useless detail, but not a single fact which could
be used as evidence against her. With remarkable ad-
roitness for a girl of her age, she disentangled herself
from the web.

Her suitor was executed in March 1549. When the
news was brought to Elizabeth, she is reported to have
coldly observed : 'This day died a man with much wit
and very little judgement.' The story comes from a
doubtful source, the historian Leti, writing in the
second half of the seventeenth century, and quoting
documents which have not survived—or which may
have been specially invented for the occasion. Yet, in
this case, there is an authentic quality about the remark.

It would not be hard to imagine it as her epitaph upon a failure.

Elizabeth may have kept her secret from her inquisitors, and from us. But other incidents suggest that, while he lived, the sophisticated and gallant Seymour had no little capacity to awaken a romantic response in Elizabeth, a capacity which he shared with only two other men throughout her life. One was Robert Dudley, Earl of Leicester. The other emerged long afterwards in the tragi-comic figure of the Duke of Alençon. But when, in personal matters, Elizabeth had made up her mind where she stood, she rarely looked back over her shoulders at the fading scene. (This was not the case with *political* matters : but that is another story.) When Seymour was in disgrace, or dead, she would have no difficulty in writing him off, if his memory in any way handicapped her in negotiating a passage through the cross-currents of political intrigue.

During the remainder of Edward VI's reign, England was tossed about amid the squalid manoeuvres of a divided government without a mature king to guide it. It is an apt commentary upon factious rule that the Protector who had sent his brother to the Tower in January 1549 was himself a prisoner there before the year was out. His enemy, Warwick, who ousted him, was a more resolute man, whose limitless ambition was sustained by a ruthless and inflexible will. His hold over the young king was complete. The same was not true of his hold over the nation; and he knew it. So, as the boy grew sick, Warwick, now Duke of Northumberland, made the desperate decision to retain control of the state by diverting the succession from the main Henrician line to Lady Jane Grey (married to Northumberland's son, Guilford Dudley). On Edward's death he removed from the succession by one stroke Mary, the lawful queen, and Elizabeth, her heir. But in two short weeks he saw power and hope trickle away through his fingers as political opinion swung sharply in favour of the elder daughter of Henry VIII. On July 20, 1553, Northumberland accepted the inevitable and made the wan gesture of himself throwing his hat in the air as he proclaimed Mary Queen of England.

On August 3, 1553, Mary rode in triumph through the London streets. At her side was her half-sister Elizabeth, at that time a month short of her twentieth birthday.

Mary at 37 was nearly twice Elizabeth's age; and mental strain and recurrent sickness had made her older than her years. But it was not merely eighteen years which separated them. The difference lay in a whole attitude to life. Each, it is true, had the Tudor sense of monarchy and calling. Each had superb courage in the face of violence or the threat of violence. And there the resemblance ended. A Spanish mother gave Mary an obstinate and unquestioning faith in her church and its ultimate triumph; while the memory of her mother's experiences had twisted her soul into the agonized shape of a fanatic. Elizabeth had no memory of her mother and was herself uncommitted, in the fullest sense, to any creed. While Mary never doubted her religious mission, Elizabeth was not conscious of having one. Mary thought that there was only one road to heaven, along which her subjects must be led or driven for the sake of their immortal souls. Elizabeth believed that in her Father's house there were many mansions.

The Londoners must have been struck by the contrast between the two sisters as they drove into the capital on that August day in 1553. Yet the differences between them—in appearance, religion and policy—concealed one bond which joined them, and which was never broken. At times Mary thought of trying to oust her from the succession. But in the end she recognized that, if she died childless, her only heir must be Elizabeth. Yet in the early years her advisors, especially her foreign ones, urged her that Elizabeth was the greatest menace to the nation and its faith, and that she must be destroyed. Had Mary acted on this advice then, within the terms of the *realpolitik* of the age, it would have been hard to condemn her. But if Elizabeth had been executed, the next heir would have been Mary Stuart, her second cousin. She was a Catholic, Elizabeth was a Protestant. But Mary Stuart was a Scottish queen, closely allied to France. Her succession would have meant either the submergence of England under French dominance, or its break-up into civil war. In the choice between attempting to safeguard her religion under Catholic Mary Queen of Scots, or safeguarding the integrity of the Tudor succession (and therefore the independence of England) under Protestant Elizabeth,

Mary Tudor put the integrity of the succession first. It is well to remember this of her when the charges of bigotry and bloodthirstiness are made. There is an historical irony in the situation. By a stroke of the pen Mary might have cut short Elizabeth Tudor's career before it began. But in fact it was Catholic Mary who made the country safe for Anglican Protestantism.

Mary proved at the last the great protectress of Elizabeth : no easy task. For within six months of Mary's accession, Sir Thomas Wyatt, a Kentish gentleman, son of the poet, put English opinion to the test by leading a powerful force on London. The immediate cause was not the change in religion—though that may have brought some men to his banner—but the announcement of the imminent marriage of the queen to her cousin, Philip II of Spain. Mary was the first queen regnant of England, but it looked as though she would inaugurate her rule by renouncing it, that she would give up her sovereignty in order to add yet another satellite to the Spanish Hapsburg Empire. It was that, not religion, which brought her subjects to arms. 'We are all Englishmen,' cried one body of the queen's troops as they went over to the support of Wyatt. It was a near thing. For a moment it looked as though the whole Marian governing class would crumble. But, after a violent shudder, it recovered, and the capital itself, when finally tested, stood firmly with the queen. Wyatt was taken prisoner. With him in their hands the government tried to trace the long trail of conspiracy back to its source, which they believed lay in

Elizabeth herself. If that was so, they never found it.

Whatever Wyatt may have let slip in the early stages, at the end he wholly acquitted her of any part in the affair. This saved her from the scaffold, but it could not save her from the Tower. On the whole, we are inclined to believe Elizabeth's firm assertions of her innocence. She was not the kind of person to 'jump the gun'; to commit herself to rebellion while the outcome was still uncertain. If the rebels succeeded, she was their obvious candidate. If they failed, then she could not sweeten defeat for them by sacrificing her life for a lost cause.

Rebellion taught Elizabeth the virtues of discretion. But it taught Mary nothing. She pressed on with the marriage project as if in fulfilment of a mission. She would cancel the humiliations inflicted on her Spanish mother by crowning a Spaniard king of England. She would give birth to an heir—but for this time was short —who would one day rule Catholic England as part of a Hapsburg Empire. Marry Philip she did: but she lived only long enough to see the grand illusion evaporate before her eyes. Philip II never loved her. He came only twice and his visits were too short for him to get used either to the tedium of the English court or the rigours of the northern climate. The heir whom Mary at one stage thought she carried turned out to be one more manifestation of a long-standing disease. And the English forces dragged their heels when called upon to play their part in Spanish imperialistic adventures. Meanwhile Elizabeth, released from the Tower, lived in the shadows; but each day made her inheritance more certain. And she knew it.

Before long, Mary also must have known it. And she would do nothing to prevent Elizabeth from claiming her own. But Mary must at least ensure that the England to which Elizabeth succeeded was free from the Protestant taint. In that case the Protestant queen would be bound to acknowledge, as an established fact, that England was, and would always remain, Catholic. In Smithfield and Oxford and in the little towns of provincial England, the fires consumed the Protestant martyrs; but these ghastly ceremonies were a sign, not that Mary was bloodthirsty, but that she had lost confidence in herself. For now she knew that she would have no heir. These ritual murders displayed the neurotic idealism of a dying queen, hoping vainly by a last service to her country to reunite it with Catholic Christendom.

The headlong rush to dispose of heretics—religious or political—is always a clear sign of a government's failure of nerve. But we may assume too readily in this case that it was a hopeless task. Heresy had been wiped out in the past by fire and sword. Soon it would be stamped out again in some parts of central Europe—in places where it seemed to have achieved a powerful hold. Mary was not to know that traditional and well-tried weapons for destroying heresy would snap in her hands. On the contrary, had she lived long enough, her life's mission might have been fulfilled. But the unmistakable intimations of her mortality gave a frenzy to her zeal. It gave also a memory to persecution which it took centuries to obliterate. She passed on to her sister a divided realm.

The rapidly changing political scene during these formative years of Elizabeth's life played an enormous part in shaping her whole policy as queen. Over and over again she had seen the unity and integrity of England jeopardized. The policies of Henry VIII in precipitating the Reformation, of Edward VI in allying with one extremist minority and of Mary in allying with another, all these threatened to disrupt England as a nation and leave her, as Scotland would shortly be left, the weak dependency of a powerful neighbour. That fear dominated the political horizon of Elizabeth; and, if there was any consistent thread running through her whole outlook, it was the desire to safeguard the unity of England, at any cost, against the enormous dangers which beset it from within and without.

Now, with more than a lifetime of experience crowded into twenty-five years, Elizabeth waited at Hatfield for the news which she knew could not be long delayed; and in the early hours of November 17, 1558, Mary died. At once the advisors, the politicians, the friends of the new queen took the road north out of London to Hatfield, and they came well supplied with principles and policies, if she would be willing to listen to them. But at about this time it was a poet, speaking as a bridegroom and in the name of England, who perhaps best conveyed the national mood as he welcomed her to the capital :

> *I am thy lover fair,*
> *Hath chose thee to mine heir,*
> *And my name is Merrie England.*
> *Therefore, come away*
> *And make no more delay.*
> *Sweet Bessie give me thy hand.*

It had been a long, discreet wooing ; but, at last, it was over.

Chapter Two

The Opening of an Age, 1558

'IT appears to me', said the Spanish Ambassador in London of the Princess Elizabeth, a week before her accession to the throne, 'that she is a woman of extreme vanity, but acute.' When it had become clear to him that Queen Mary's life was ebbing fast, he had sought an interview with Elizabeth, as the heir apparent, and had found her cordial, though hardly effusive. But when the ambassador was so bold as to suggest that she owed her present survival and future prospects to her Spanish brother-in-law, Philip, she bluntly answered that the people of England had placed her where she was. In saying that, she was probably sincere. It is true that the 'people', had not been consulted; nor, of course, did any electoral machinery exist for discovering the will of the people as a whole. But this was another of her ways of saying that she was 'mere English'; that she believed that the roots of the Tudor monarchy lay in the English nation; that she placed no hope whatsoever in foreign promises or foreign troops. If this was her code she clung to it throughout her life.

English indeed she was; and with a characteristic mixture of races and classes. From her father's side Elizabeth drew the royal blood of both York and Lancaster; but it was mingled also with the Tudor blood of

the Welsh gentry. On her mother's side she derived
from the aristocratic Howards, Dukes of Norfolk; but
they in their turn had married into the merchant
family of the Boleyns. It was a happy—and symbolic
—juncture of the old with the new. There still exists, at
Hatfield House, a pedigree of Queen Elizabeth which
traces her back, quite correctly, to William the Con-
queror; and beyond that, after many generations, to
Adam and Eve. At that stage her pedigree may be a
little faulty according to the exacting standards of
modern historical research. But what is beyond dispute
is that her royal and aristocratic blood had something
in it from the middling gentry of the shires as well as a
touch of the cockney pride of Sir Geoffrey Boleyn, her
great-grandfather, sometime Lord Mayor of London.

The weeks after her accession were busy ones, with
ministers to be appointed, policies to be examined,
dispatches to be read—all this amid the preparations
for the coronation. And then, after two hectic months,
on Thursday, January 12, 1559, she entered the Tower
of London. This was not the first sojourn she had made
within its inhospitable walls; but now the auspices were
better. For, in keeping with custom, she would pass a
few days there on her way to be crowned.

On the following Saturday she made her formal
entry into the city of London; and it became quickly
evident to all that she, no less than her subjects, delighted in all the rich pageantry of the age. Pomp
indeed was what they wanted. But it was in her little
touches of intimacy with her common subjects that

this great-granddaughter of Alderman Boleyn felt her way into their hearts—a friendly word here, the ready acceptance of some humble gift there. Still, she sacrificed no fraction of her regality; and, when someone in the crowd called out: 'Remember old King Henry VIII', a comprehending smile was seen to pass across her face.

It is not surprising that, at this time in her life, her features recalled those of her father. She was somewhat above the average height and well-proportioned. Her hair was a reddish-gold, naturally wavy, and her full round face, with its light skin, made her dark piercing eyes seem all the more penetrating. It was undoubtedly a Tudor face; and it is understandable that, for the moment, the watching Londoners should feel that Henry VIII was again in their midst.

But if we are to understand the mind and attitudes of Elizabeth, we should look not only at the Holbein portraits of Henry VIII but at the effigy of Henry VII in the crypt of Westminster Abbey. For, as the years passed, her face would grow leaner, the high cheekbones more pronounced, the features—and the tongue —sharper. The historian who looks at her portraits— and her policies—later in the reign sees in them less of Henry VIII, her father, and more of Henry VII, her grandfather. That was perhaps a fortunate thing, for it was his policies—economy and caution rather than political adventures—that the times required.

The following day, on Sunday, January 15, the queen went with all solemnity to her coronation at

Westminster Abbey. This, the processions and the en-
tertainments were manifestly as pleasurable to the
queen as to her subjects; and her boundless vivacity
responded to the buoyant moods of the day. But
England on holiday was not quite the same thing as
England at work; and this small but growing nation
soon presented the new queen with some tough problems crying out for solution.

The exact size of the nation at that time we do not
precisely know. Nor have we any serious prospect of
ever discovering it. Out of a series of estimates, made
by contemporaries and historians, we should probably
not be far wrong if we said that, at the beginning of
the reign, it was less than one-tenth of what it is today
and, at the end of the reign, somewhat more than one-
tenth. A broad guess would take us somewhere between
three and five millions. The population was undoubtedly growing, but it was far, far less than that of France.
It is worth recalling also that, for the first time since
the Norman Conquest, England was without a single
acre of territory in France. The end of Mary's reign
saw the end of the English empire (in France). To
some it must have seemed also the end of England's
greatness as well. It proved instead the creative pause
before the opening of a time of true greatness. *Reculer
pour mieux sauter*!—a recurrent pattern in English
history.

Yet Elizabeth's greatest problem lay not across the
Channel but at home, and in the pockets of the people.
For, during the two decades preceding her accession,

England had passed through a severe wave of inflation,
unparalleled until our own day. The frequent debase-
ments of the currency, and the increased supply of
precious metals from the New World, poured money
into circulation. This, moreover, occurred at a time
when the rising population was pushing ahead, especially in southern England, of the nation's capacity to
produce. The result was a tearaway rise in prices, an
unstable boom in trade (as the pound's value fell
abroad), social discontent and distress. Drastic defla-
tionary steps were taken by the new government in
1560–1 which, although they could not stop inflation
in its tracks, sharply reduced the inflationary pace. This
was followed, in 1563, by a second bid for economic
stability of which one manifestation was the celebrated
Statute of Artificers: an attempt to hold industry and
labour within their accustomed channels. The prospect
of social stability came into view; but success was
necessarily limited and uneven in the scattered com-
munities of Elizabethan England.

The few millions of people occupying these islands
were indeed spread pretty thinly upon the ground. It is
true that there were great centres of population; ports
like Bristol, Hull, Newcastle and, pre-eminently,
London; cloth towns like Beverley, Norwich and Salis-
bury; cathedral cities like York, Winchester and Exeter.
Busy and crowded centres of industry, trade, administration they undoubtedly were, but they were all
within sight of green fields and, with the exception of

London, the greatest of them were rarely larger than a medium-sized market town of today.

It was a country small in size but diverse in its peoples. The northern counties were still something of a political no-man's-land, where border warfare was endemic, life brutal and justice uncertain in its incidence but barbarous in its execution. Further south, Yorkshire and Lancashire were more settled; but the social structure still bore the marks of late medieval feudalism. The people looked to the local lord, and the older religion, rather than to the central power (or its delegate, the Lord President of the Council in the North) or the new church. The midlands and the south had more in common with each other and with the queen's government in London; but away to the southwest there were many signs of a rugged peninsular independence, to be channelled later on into the aggressive exploits of Elizabethan seamen.

Wales, too, was part of the queen's dominions; and it provided throughout the period a remarkable instance of unity in diversity. Her people spoke a different tongue from the queen's English; her mountains emphasized her isolation and safeguarded her culture. The (somewhat remote) Welsh ancestry of the queen may have exercised a pull the other way; but, more important, the Welsh political sense—*tacte des choses possibles*—and their genius for assimilation speedily made them loyal subjects of Elizabeth I. In Ireland, by contrast, there was a tragic story of division : division of people, of religion, of political loyalty. She was already the victim of the blunders of history. There was little confidence or goodwill between the two nations, separated as they were by the Irish Channel and by so much else : an intractable problem for Elizabeth I and all her successors.

The queen's capital was growing fast. Every square yard of land was being built on. Existing houses were divided and subdivided into squalid tenements. Upper storeys were added, each one reaching out a little further into the middle of the road. By the time that the fifth storey was put on the inhabitants of opposite sides of the road could shake hands—or quarrel—without moving from their seats by the window.

The government was greatly worried by the continuous flow of a very miscellaneous collection of people to the capital, some drawn to the hundreds of trades flourishing—on and off—in the city; some looking for domestic employment in the town houses of the great; some looking for mischief—cut-throats, pickpockets and prostitutes. Then, as now, few citizens of the metropolis could claim, on both sides of the family, a London ancestry to the second generation.

An angry Recorder of London once drew up a long list of sturdy vagabonds he had laid by the heels in one of the sudden swoops made by the city government. He found among them not a single one who had been born in the capital. They had all been sucked in from the four corners of the kingdom. 'London cannot relieve England,' cried another social critic as he threw his hands up in despair. The capital was the great melting-

pot of the English—as well as of the Welsh and Irish—
and there were even a few Scotsmen, still members of
a foreign nation, who found the city somewhat agree-
able to their tastes and ambitions.

The government embarked on a policy of slum clear-
ance; but with only statutes and exhortations as their
weapons. They failed. But, where they failed, plague
and disease took a hand in the proceedings and deci-
mated the population by thousands in a few months.
For many people the London life was a short and
squalid one. But still they came : not only the poor but
the middling and upper classes, with their families and
servants. Some came as lawyers, others as Members of
Parliament and others formed part of that great 'establishment', the court circle, by which must be understood not only the gilded splendour of palace life but
the power, influence and high and dangerous stakes
of the whole Elizabethan political world. In sharp contrast with the turbulent poverty of their fellow citizens,
the families of the governing classes could live in luxury
and at ease. By the end of the reign it was the fashion
for anyone of social standing to be driven about the
town in his own coach and horses, with the result that
the traffic jams in central London threatened, on occasion, to bring life to a standstill.

But the majority of the queen's subjects dwelt neither
in London, nor in the provincial cities, but in the
countryside; and here too there was considerable diversity. Over a large part of England—more especially in
the central plain—men still cultivated the open fields,

where their methods reflected the long centuries of tradition. But often enough during the past fifty years the growing flocks of sheep had brought a wool prosperity—and sometimes a wool depression—to those farmers who had moved from corn to pasture. In the process the way of life and the social framework were changing.

For example, a yeoman farmer might prosper and climb into the gentry, or live to see his son do so. Nor was it impossible for a yeoman's grandson to take the first bold step into the peerage. There were new and old gentry, new and old aristocracy. As often in our history, an impoverished nobleman brushed up his family escutcheon with merchant gold, by the discreet marriage of his heir into the trading classes. In the countryside as in the capital, great wealth and great poverty could exist side by side. But again as today, countryfolk somehow enjoyed as a community a greater cohesion than did townspeople. An intruding landlord who bought up the estate of a decaying gentleman would, it is true, in the first generation have the accents and the postures of a different world. But soon his roots would grow close to those of his neighbours and, as the years passed, his family tomb in the parish church would show that in the end he had come to stay.

But the whole countryside was not given over to either corn or sheep. The textile industry was, in many respects, still a country industry, in Yorkshire, Gloucestershire and elsewhere. Timber-cutting, also, went on in many districts, and there were anxieties, exaggerated as they turned out to be, that a timber famine lay just around the corner. Coal was being mined and was increasingly used as a domestic fuel, bringing comforts—as well as discomforts—of its own : as the Londoners were coming to recognize as they coughed and spluttered in the wintry fog. But it would be a long time before coal ousted timber in either the fireplaces or the industries of England. A little later in the reign copper and zinc would be mined, but not enough to repair the fortunes of those who had plunged too much capital in the ventures. In many other ways the English countryman was learning new arts and crafts as well as changing the techniques of old ones. At the same time English seamen fished from a hundred ports as well as probed for routes to empire in the New World, then still dominated by the Iberian powers. In all spheres, but most of all on the high seas, Elizabethan Englishmen displayed a vigour and independence which would make them resourceful alike as allies and enemies.

One day their independence of mood would strike at the old queen herself. Indeed, her inaugural years already gave more than one sign of the breakers which lay ahead, especially so in the matter of religion, for in this the queen and her subjects must shortly make up their minds where they stood. If the queen hesitated—and she had good reasons for doing so—then she ran the risk that her subjects might make up her mind for her.

In the quarter of a century before her succession

England underwent a number of sharp changes in religion. This is not a sign that Englishmen were fickle. On the contrary, the majority of them watched without commitment the battle over doctrine and policy in high places and, with characteristic phlegm, shrugged their shoulders. Like Elizabeth Tudor herself, and her future minister, William Cecil, they conformed. A whole generation of mid-Tudor England, apart from a vigorous minority, swam with the rapidly changing religious tides which flowed from London.

A Spanish ambassador, in the early years of the dynasty, had made the harsh comment that Englishmen did not know the difference between the Bible and the Koran. He misjudged them. He mistook lack of outward passion for lack of feeling. Englishmen hate to wear their hearts—or their religion—on their sleeves. They tend to be orthodox without clinging tenaciously to any particular dogma. Their creed, as is still manifested in the whole *ethos* of the Church of England, has great spiritual force but is also flexible and expansive. They might therefore understand Henri IV of France when he said that to gain Paris he would go to Mass; in other words, that national interest came before dogma. They found it less easy to understand his daughter, Henrietta Maria, wife of Charles I of England, for in her view creed should be the master of policy. And Henri IV's grandson, James II of England, frankly baffled and alarmed them. For he lost London in the hope of restoring the Mass.

The majority conformed. But religious intensity and

extremism, if rare plants in England, can on occasion be very sturdy ones. The average Tudor Englishman who lived out his years in conformity probably admired, as we do, the sharp vision of the martyr who could see no other way to salvation than the laying down of his life for a dogma. But admiration fell short of imitation. In twos and threes the idealists proudly went to their deaths in the market squares of London and provincial England; but there were no religious wars in the sixteenth century. The 'Puritan' civil wars of the middle of the seventeenth century have long since broken out of that straitjacket of a title. But the Hebrew prophet who long ago spoke of a 'righteous remnant' of his own race whose influence would far outweigh its numbers, might well have been speaking also of the passionate minorities of mid-Tudor England. Under Edward VI the Catholics saw all that they believed in swept away; but a section of them never acknowledged defeat. Under Mary, the Protestants showed that they had a passionate minority who would burn or go into exile rather than jeopardize their immortal souls through compromise.

Elizabeth had not been one of these. Nor had William Cecil, her Secretary of State; nor Thomas Parry, her cofferer; least of all the pliant William Paulet, Marquess of Winchester who, as he said, was carved out of the willow, not the oak. Many of his colleagues in Elizabeth's Privy Council were hewn of the same timber. So were many of her subjects.

But the problems of history are not caused by the

average man with the average views. It needs only two vigorous minorities, confident in the righteousness of their cause, to split a country from top to bottom. In 1558 the inherent contradictions in a situation which had lasted for thirty years were fully revealed. And for the first time the throne was occupied by a monarch who was not prepared to throw in her lot with one side and stamp hard on the other. Edward VI and Mary had only one opposition to contend with, Catholic or Protestant; Elizabeth had both. To walk in the middle of the road, in religion and politics, is sometimes thought to be prudent. But it has hazards of its own. One runs the risk of being knocked down by fast traffic coming from either direction.

Looking back on Elizabeth's reign—and considering it mainly in political terms—one can see that her policy paid very high dividends. It was therefore at one time thought that all this belonged to a grand design on the part of Elizabeth and some of her advisors, who rightly judged that what England needed was a tranquil interlude of moderation, so that the great, uncommitted majority of Englishmen could live and work in peace. The Acts of Supremacy and Uniformity of 1559, and the Thirty-Nine Articles which followed in 1563, gave England a church which was Catholic in structure (without the Pope), and in ceremonial (without the Mass), but Calvinist in much of its doctrine and insular in its outlook. That was the Anglican Settlement. But Elizabeth, Professor Neale has shown, had hoped to retain a considerable measure of her father's church,

which was much more Catholic in doctrine than the
Protestant churches of Europe. Whatever filial piety
there was in this was strongly reinforced by her political
outlook and by her desire not to offend the powerful
Catholic princes of Europe.

Her most vociferous subjects, however, looked the
other way, especially those who had, during Mary's
reign, gone in search of continental Protestantism and
had liked what they had found. At one stage, in 1559,
it appeared that Elizabeth might come into conflict
with the more dogmatic of her Protestant subjects.
Then the whole situation seemed to change and she
swung round to meet her opponents half-way. As in
other crises of her reign, Elizabeth did not start off with
any clear solution in mind but rescued compromise out
of a dangerous situation.

So far as we can tell, Elizabeth was the only Tudor
monarch who held no strong views on religion. Such
views as she did hold were expressed negatively rather
than positively. She objected particularly to some of
the more elaborate ceremonials of the old church. The
lighted tapers of the Abbot of Westminster, as he
greeted her at the opening of her first parliament, were
met with a rebuke which must have seemed to him
and the assembled monks a dark symbol of the new
age: 'Away with those torches! We can see well
enough!' She objected to the elevation of the host at
Mass. She objected, as she told the Spanish Ambassador, to her subjects' money going out of England to
supply the pope. She objected—but in this she was not

successful—to her bishops alleviating their ecclesiastical
and political burdens with the delights of matrimony.

But if her objections to clerical marriage derived in
part from the traditional theology she inherited from
her father, her hostility touched also something much
deeper in her personality. Indeed, the whole question
of her own marriage raised such complex, profound
and dangerous issues that her ministers—as well as later
historians—lived to see their own solutions to the riddle
disappear without trace in the quicksands of a woman's
mood. But this problem of her marriage lies at the core
of any interpretation of Elizabethan policy. We must
therefore turn to it, even though it involves extending
the borders of history a little into the open fields of
speculation.

Chapter Three

Suitors for the Queen, 1559–62

ELIZABETH'S ministers and subjects from the start assumed that she would soon take a husband. For who could be expected to guess that she would be the only woman ruler in English history who did not marry? Certainly she was not short of suitors. So august a person as Philip II of Spain assuaged his grief for his dead wife, Mary, by declaring himself ready to marry Elizabeth, on the assumption that the pope would grant a dispensation to enable him to marry his deceased wife's sister. Elizabeth, with tactful irony, replied that she anticipated difficulty in obtaining such a dispensation; and, in the stylized language of diplomacy, shook off a prospect which can have aroused in her nothing but revulsion.

These feelings were no doubt shared by a considerable body of public and parliamentary opinion, not least by the protagonists of a forward-looking protestantism deeply hostile to Spain. But, if the House of Commons would have viewed with alarm the reappearance of Philip II as a king-consort, its members were no less alarmed at the prospect that Elizabeth might delay marriage too long and, amidst the swift hazards of plague or rebellion, die without heir. In that case, one of two things would happen. Either Mary,

Queen of Scots, married to the Dauphin, would succeed, in which case England would have exchanged the Catholic-Spanish domination of Mary Tudor for the Catholic-French domination of Mary Stuart. Or her succession would be challenged by one or more claimants, in which case England would enter upon the Wars of the Roses, stage two. Whatever happened, the protestant settlement, so recently refounded by the faithful, might in the ensuing confusion be lost beyond recall. To this problem the Commons devoted their ripening wisdom and their fervent pressure.

They were met by that ambiguous rhetoric of which the queen was already showing herself a master. Whenever God decided that she should marry, she replied, marry she would: and it would be prudently and profitably for the state. If God decided instead that she should not marry, then she would accept her fate equably, while at the same time ensuring for her realm a worthy successor. In that case she offered her Commons the further consolation of one day surveying her marble monument proclaiming that she 'lived and died a virgin'. After which assurance she proceeded, with gay abandon, to reject the suits of about a dozen candidates, including the Crown Prince of Sweden and a couple of Austrian archdukes.

But to the parliamentarians, marriage seemed an indispensable guarantee to their security. For the survival of their religion was inextricably bound up with the survival of the régime: and Elizabeth was the last of her line. All that she must herself have recognized.

Yet some impassable barrier stood against the fulfilment of her subjects'—and perhaps her own—most
earnest desire. How, then, are we to explain, with the
historical data at our disposal (both inadequate and
contradictory), why Elizabeth lived and died a virgin?

It is quite possible that, from the start, Elizabeth
knew that marriage was out of the question, because
some consuming disease which Henry VIII carried in
his veins made his children either sick or sterile. Some
contemporaries believed that Elizabeth was fully aware
all the time of a major physical disability which pre-
cluded for ever the normal married life. Marriage
itself would therefore be ruled out, for it would bring
her only a companion on the throne—perhaps even a
master—yet never the object of marriage : an heir. But
she could still use *negotiations* for marriage as part of
the diplomatic game. In other words she could involve
herself over and over again in marriage schemes, secure
in the knowledge that the citadel would never fall.
Marriage projects would end as they began : in a series
of diplomatic manoeuvres.

There is much to recommend this thesis, for it would
give to her policies a coherence which it is otherwise
not easy to discover. But it is, unfortunately, a thesis
which cannot be securely held. Her own doctor once
gave the French Ambassador the strongest assurance
that Elizabeth could bear ten children. William Cecil
who, apart from her doctor, was probably in the best
position to speak, declared that 'nature cannot amend
her shape in any part to make her more likely to con-

ceive and bear children without peril'. This may be the dubious evidence of the politician, but we know that there were at least two occasions, as we shall see, when it seemed certain that Elizabeth would marry; and both times she was stayed, not by her own reluctance, but by the strong hostility of her ministers and subjects. We must set this, therefore, against assertions of her sterility by her enemies, eager to jump at the first adverse theory to hand, and against, also, the dim recollections of an old, loquacious ambassador alleging that she once described herself as a barren stock. For a women to reach the age of 25 without being married was, in those days, enough to stimulate surprise and suspicion. Some of Elizabeth's contemporaries were twice widowed and thrice married before their twenty-fifth birthday. To reach 45 in the celibate state could arouse nothing short of astonishment. It seemed to many that, for this unnatural condition, there could be no other explanation but physical disability.

Yet such conclusions are insecurely founded because the sources are, necessarily, so defective. Even more defective is the material for writing the inward, emotional history of the queen. Yet it may be that, for her, psychological barriers against marriage proved even more unyielding than any physical ones which may have existed.

Her own mother's marriage, as she knew, had been built on the rupture of her father's first marriage to Katharine of Aragon. And shortly her mother's marriage had ended on the block. Her mother's supplanter,

Jane Seymour, had died young in childbirth. Her successor, Anne of Cleves, had been bundled out of wedlock with indecorous speed. Henry's fifth wife, Katharine Howard, had followed in Anne Boleyn's footsteps to the block. His sixth wife, Katharine Parr, had survived him only to die in childbirth shortly after her remarriage. Elizabeth's sister, Mary, had gained in marriage only false hopes and dragging despair. The attempt to marry her brother, Edward VI, to the young Mary, Queen of Scots, had been drenched in blood at the battle of Pinkie. Certainly, there was nothing in the marital experiences of Elizabeth's father, mother, stepmothers or sister to encourage an unduly optimistic view of matrimony; while her own experiences at the hands of Thomas Seymour had brought a brief excitement and a dangerous threat.

There had followed ten years of dissimulation as she passed from girlhood to womanhood, with every display of affection watched by a thousand eyes, every true emotion corked up within her. It would have been strange indeed if, after all this, Elizabeth had been capable of giving a straight answer to all the pressing questions, personal and public, of her marriage. The same discord seemed to intervene in her attitude to marriage in general. Throughout her life, as she watched the young people about her court develop warm and romantic attachments, they would arouse in her a hostility, more bitter and remorseless than when far larger issues offended her. So love at court perforce became clandestine. It was as though she realized that she would never be able to give or receive the normal affections; as though twenty-five years of disillusionment and enforced deception had damaged her soul beyond the reach of private love. It may be this which made her all the more want, as she said, to dwell in the hearts of *all* her subjects.

Even so, her inward mood and policy remains something of an enigma. We are on safer ground if we consider her marriage in terms of public policy. Here alone there were many good reasons why she should hesitate before plunging into matrimony. The public consequences of her sister's marriage could, by itself, have deterred the most ardent of women. For her the position was at least as delicate. If she married a Catholic archduke, she would certainly compromise her position with her more extreme Protestant supporters at home, who might object to going on their travels again. If she married a Protestant prince of Sweden, then this diplomatic alignment would offend the great Catholic powers of Europe who, if they could ever temporarily sink their differences, might unite long enough to crush her.

If, on the other hand, she married an Englishman, then she would have to choose from one or other of the leading factions and, in tilting the scale in favour of one of them, would arouse uneasiness and perhaps resistance among all the rest. There was no shortage of suitors but, amid such an embarrassment of riches, she might well think it prudent to walk alone. In these early years Elizabeth always tried, as far as was possible, to be *politically* and *religiously* uncommitted; and she wanted all the world to know it. Her refusal to be committed in *marriage* fits in coherently with the rest of her policy at this time.

But her decision to remain celibate—if it was a decision and not the gradual recognition that for her there was no other way—involved something of a gamble. It was a gamble that she would live long enough to pass on a stable England, firmly established, united in religion and politics, to a known and undisputed successor. But if she lost the gamble and died young, then England could hardly hope to escape a war over the succession. In other words, if she married, England might be faced with one kind of war; if she did not, with another. It was a situation which encouraged vacillation, ambiguity—and virginity. In many ways it satisfied the temperament of the young queen.

It is quite possible, however, that none of these analyses really explains her abstention from marriage and that the true explanation is the simplest of them all. Elizabeth was a career-woman. She knew and loved the arts of government. Marriage and motherhood would deprive her temporarily—perhaps permanently—of the authority and power to rule. To share power she would hate. To renounce it she would find intolerable. 'I will have here,' she once stormed at Robert Dudley, 'but one mistress and no master.' As happens in every generation, some able women come to believe—rightly or wrongly—that marriage and a career are incompatible. 'Madam, I know your stately stomach,' said a Scottish ambassador to her, 'ye think that if ye were married ye would be but Queen of England, and now ye are King and Queen both. Ye may not suffer a commander.' Only a foreigner dared say such a thing to the queen; and perhaps he was right.

Yet in spite of this, there were times when all her rational opposition to her own marriage looked like being blown away in a sudden gust of emotion. At last, it seemed she would marry. Then the mood would pass; policy would conquer instinct. She accepted what she believed was the logic of the situation and resumed her statecraft. The unity of England (which her own marriage might destroy) she loved more deeply than the procession of suitors who came and saw—but never conquered.

Yet there was, in these early days, one man who could arouse in her sufficient emotion to threaten havoc to the emergent Elizabethan policy. He was Robert Dudley; and, for his sake, all the formidable arguments against marriage seemed for a while to be held in suspense.

That Elizabeth fell in love with Dudley there can be no doubt; but when that happened we cannot be sure. Perhaps it was when they met at the court of her brother, Edward VI, when she and Robert were both sixteen. Later on, during Mary's reign, they were in the Tower, she under suspicion because of Wyatt's rebellion, he under sentence of death because of his complicity in the plot of his father, the Duke of North-

umberland, to displace Mary. His father and brother
were executed; and Elizabeth and Robert must each
have measured, in the mind's eye, the short distance
from the Tower to the block. But they probably never
met. Later both were free; and, in the last year of
Mary's reign, while she waited at Hatfield for her inheritance, he restored his family name by giving a good
account of himself as a soldier of the dying queen.
Then, with Elizabeth's accession, they met again; and
he became a firm favourite.

Gossip at once put their relations on a more intimate
basis. In the summer of 1560 a woman in Essex was
sent to prison for saying that Elizabeth was with child
and that its father was Robert Dudley. In various parts
of the country other purveyors of fantasies finished up
in the same place; but gaol could not silence a rumour,
the echoes of which would go rumbling on through
history. Yet, whatever their personal relations, of one
thing we can be reasonably certain : Elizabeth wanted
to marry Dudley. He had so much to commend him :
he was handsome, gallant, of her own generation and
experience. But two things barred the way. The first
was the bitter hostility of other courtiers against him. A
divided court could temporarily unite, and even intrigue with a foreign ambassador, to thwart so baleful
a match. The waxing and the waning of these fears
are to be read right through the correspondence of
the period. There was a second, and even greater,
impediment to the match; for Dudley had married
Amy Robsart in the middle of Edward VI's reign.

Marriage in the sixteenth century—as in other centuries—was not necessarily an impregnable barrier to a second marriage by one of the parties. For the first wedlock could be dissolved by the legal process of annulment. It could also be dissolved by death. Rumour indeed stated that there was a plan afoot to murder Amy Robsart. Cecil, in a moment of calculated indiscretion, repeated it to the Spanish ambassador. And then, to confirm the worst, on September 8, 1560, she was found dead at the foot of a flight of stairs at Cumnor Place in Berkshire. Dudley was implicated; so therefore was Elizabeth. Here seemed the most damning evidence of a royal adulteress advancing to the marriage altar with blood on her hands.

Yet an examination of the evidence deprives it of its force; and the coroner's jury rejected it, returning instead a verdict of accidental death. The jury may have been corrupted, or terrified, or both. But, even so, there is very much which supports them. On the day of her death Amy, clearly a sick woman, did her best to get her friends and servants away from the house. She would hardly do this in anticipation of murder. But of suicide? Much ink has been spilt from that day to this on every fragment of evidence that has survived about the case. The latest opinion, that of a leading medical authority, suggests that for Amy, already in an advanced stage of malignant illness, even a slight fall would have broken her neck. Moreover, in her mortal condition, and with her husband's affections gone for ever, she may have felt that the only way out lay in suicide.

It has been said that her death 'undoubtedly removed the chief obstacle to the marriage of the queen with Dudley'. It did nothing of the kind. If Amy Robsart, while she lived, made the queen's marriage difficult, in her death—and the manner of her death—she made it impossible. Elizabeth still behaved as though a marriage with Dudley were practicable but, as time passed, she began to accept the logic of the situation. A diplomat, at the beginning of 1560, had described Dudley as 'the king that is to be'. He spoke wildly. Elizabeth would go on showing Dudley her deep affection, would shower office and honour upon him, including the earldom of Leicester in 1564. But to marry him, she came to see, would divide her council and her country, in which the opposition to the match could be more fierce even than anything encountered by her sister Mary, when she married Philip II of Spain. And then, as her hopes of marriage faded, she proceeded—supreme irony!—to offer him as a suitor to her cousin Mary, Queen of Scots. That gesture, perhaps more than anything else in her reign, makes the historian feel that the intervening centuries between her age and ours cut off something of our understanding of her mind and policy. It may have baffled Mary, Queen of Scots, no less. In any case, she courteously declined the offer —and made a disastrous marriage elsewhere.

All that lay in the future. But even when Dudley was at the height of his influence with the queen, he was not alone in her counsels. There was one man, abler than Dudley who, though not yet middle-aged, displayed all the maturity and skill of a statesman. This, combined with an unassuageable passion for work, made him the perfect foil for Dudley and, in her quieter moods, the ideal servant of the queen. William Cecil, appointed Secretary of State at the beginning of her reign, served her for more than a decade in that exacting role and then for quarter of a century in the even more burdensome office of Lord High Treasurer of England. Like Dudley, he could claim that his father and grandfather had served the Tudors, but his family —middling gentry from the Welsh border when the century began—had never climbed to the same eminence as the Dudleys. When success came, as it did to William Cecil and his son Robert, they received it with reserve, speaking deprecatingly of their wealth and power; trying, without success, to disarm envy by saying that they were mere servants transmitting policy but never making it. Father and son, alike, were inward men whose voluminous papers, still available to us, reveal more about Elizabethan society than they do about these two men at the centre. They were patient men also, the father more than the son, and, unlike Dudley and his political heirs, they preferred the tortuous paths of diplomacy to the shining armour of war.

This division between Dudley and Cecil—roughly between the aggressive and conservative party—was implicit in their relations from the beginning of the reign. For Elizabeth inherited a war with France, which was of the Spanish making, and a fluid situation in Scotland allied, by long tradition and now by marriage, to the French enemy. From the French war Elizabeth disentangled herself in 1559 with the treaty of Cateau-Cambrésis. But Scotland, the satellite of France, proved a harder nut to crack. The regent there was the queen-mother, Mary of Guise, a Catholic. But, fortunately for England, she was faced by a strong Protestant opposition, stimulated among the great lords, as over a good part of Europe, by a greed for church lands, and set ablaze by the fiery preaching of the Calvinist minister, John Knox. The Scottish protestant movement, it is true, was to a large extent anti-monarchical; the 'Lords of the Congregation' who led it hardly needed the frank words of Knox on the subject of the monstrous regiment of women. All this could give little satisfaction to their royal patron south of the border, who must have viewed with contempt and alarm the antics of the most squalid feudal aristocracy in Europe, making their bids for spoils and power. But she had no choice : she kept their uneasy company with as good grace as she could, for she preferred Scotland to be ruled by inefficient Scots rather than over-efficient Frenchmen.

But she hated consorting with rebels and only did so because the alternative was a tightening French grip on Scotland. So step by step she sent money, munitions, ships and troops and, when all was done, she had, by July 1560, driven the French out and made Scotland safe for protestantism. The Treaty of Edinburgh, which was signed in that month, laid the main framework of

Anglo-Scottish policy for the rest of the reign, though it would be interrupted by Catholic reaction in Scotland and confused by baronial intrigue. For once, Cecil had played a bold hand and persuaded his mistress to fight for security in the north at the risk of European hostility to the Scottish war. But the risk was small. The mutual enmity of France and Spain neutralized any intention they may have had to embroil themselves in Anglo-Scottish affairs. And France, moreover, was on the brink of war between Huguenot and Catholic.

It was the tocsin of this war in 1562, at the 'Massacre of Vassy', that brought not only the French to arms but tempted Elizabeth also, on the only occasion in her life, to a military adventure. In this she did not carry Cecil with her, but Dudley shared her dreams of a reconquest of Calais and, perhaps, beyond that, of a new English empire in France. The project miscarried; and, worse still, before Elizabeth could extricate herself from the escapade the whole security, unity and peace of the country were flung into jeopardy. For, in October 1562, Elizabeth fell dangerously ill with smallpox.

Chapter Four

Religion, the Succession and the Scots, 1563–8

AS her ministers watched over Elizabeth tossing on her bed of sickness, they knew that, if the dread disease completed its fatal cycle, it would inevitably be followed by civil war, as well as war with Scotland, and perhaps an attack and occupation by France. Even Elizabeth, with all her tenacious will to live, despaired of her life at one stage and, trembling for the future of her country, begged her counsellors to appoint Robert Dudley as Protector of the Realm. She spoke frankly of her love for him, but swore that nothing had passed between them of which she need feel ashamed. Remembering the solemn moment in which she spoke the words, one is inclined to give more credence to them than to the stale repetitions of slander. But, luckily for England, her advice for the future had not to be tested. Even as Elizabeth was making the desperate recommendation for the protectorship, the disease passed its peak and she recovered.

On the morrow of her recovery, her council took stock of the dangerous situation through which the country had passed. And at the beginning of 1563, Parliament, summoned after an interval of four years, went straight to the heart of the matter. Indeed, Members did not need to wait for a formal debate. For, in his sermon *before* the opening of Parliament, that hot Puritan, Dean Alexander Nowell of St Paul's, gave voice to the uppermost thoughts of his listeners. 'All the queen's most noble ancestors have commonly had some issue to succeed them,' he reminded his congregation—which included the queen—'but Her Majesty yet none.' He drew his conclusion in words of one syllable : 'Which want is, for our sins, to be a plague unto us.' These were sledgehammer words but, lest there should be any fragment of doubt as to their meaning, he turned to Elizabeth herself and repeated them : 'The want of your marriage and issue,' he said, 'is like to prove . . . a plague,' as terrible a plague as her sister's marriage had been for the God-fearing men of England. (For Nowell, her reign had meant flight abroad.) 'If your parents had been of your mind,' he went on with impeccable logic, 'where had you been then ?' He expected no answer to his rhetorical question but could not cease from his labours until he had taken her on an imaginary tour of the tombs of her ancestors in Westminster Abbey so that she—and her parliamentarians—might not for one moment forget the mortality of man.

They did not forget. After the formalities were over, the Commons seized upon the first full day at their disposal to open a discussion about the queen's marriage. But they must have begun to realize even then that they might be wasting their time. Many suitors had come

and gone since the queen's accession and she was no
nearer wedlock, although she was by now within sight
of her thirtieth birthday. So the Commons began to
dig a second line of defence for the liberty, unity and
true religion of England.

If the queen did not marry, then the strongest claimant to the throne on her death would undoubtedly be
the one most hostile to their ideals and ambitions,
namely Mary, Queen of Scots. She was descended
from Henry VII and, on the grounds of Elizabeth's
illegitimacy, had already quartered the arms of England with her own. But the very thought of a Scottish,
Catholic, Francophile on the English throne was
enough to make Members of Parliament speechless with
rage, if speechless is the correct word to apply to that
unquenchable assembly. Elizabeth, no doubt, shared
their feelings; but she had not the slightest intention of
allowing them to nominate a successor or to disqualify
Mary. To name the heir was anathema to her. She
would never let an heir apparent come between her and
the light—or run the risk of his anticipating his inheritance by some bold stroke while she lived. Nor would
she disqualify Mary. Ever sensitive about the inviolable
rights of sovereignty, she could not endure for one
moment that a mere Parliament should raise a finger
to divert the divine hereditary succession. Nor, in any
case, could she allow the Commons to stamp upon the
delicate plant of Anglo-Scottish amity which she had
nursed so patiently since the early days of her power.

But still the Commons pressed her to nominate a

successor (that is, someone other than Mary), pleading that 'from the Conquest to this present day, the realm was never left, as now it is, without a certain heir, living and known'. The reply they received from the queen was stuffed full with pious generalities, kindly thoughts and vague promises. She also had some pointed comments to make on their temerity. 'I will not,' she told them, 'in so deep a matter wade with so shallow a wit' —a clear indication of what she thought of the shallow wits of the House of Commons, who had rushed in where the queen herself had hesitated to tread. But vague promises did not soothe their anxieties and, three weeks later, the Commons reverted to their theme. This time they got not even vague promises but the tart message that 'she willed the young heads to take example of the ancients'.

Elizabeth earned—and held—the reputation for giving the 'answer answerless', for leaving the petitioner uncertain as to whether he had received an affirmative or a negative reply. As the decades passed, the Commons recognized the trick; but they never trumped it. In the last years of her reign they sought to outwit her by changing their tactics. They began to think in terms of an open assault upon her prerogative. Again she outmanoeuvred them, or appeared to; but, in fact, the Tudor crown, as it passed to James I, never recovered from its experiences during the last years of Elizabeth's reign. Until then, the queen emerged the stronger; and, as son succeeded father in the House of Commons, she continued to seek her conquests over them, as women will, now with smiles, now almost in tears.

This fantastic relationship lasted for over forty years; but, of course, she held more than love-tricks in her armoury of defence. She alone possessed the power to summon and dissolve Parliament; a pertinacious assembly, which thought it could manage the queen's business better than she could herself, could be prorogued for months, or dissolved altogether. That weapon she used more than once; but it was a two-edged sword which could strike back at the queen. If she did without Parliament, then she must do without parliamentary taxation. For the usual purpose for which Parliaments were summoned throughout the Tudor period was to grant revenue. The primary function of Members of Parliament—in the eyes of the queen—was to commit their constituencies to pay taxes. It was no wonder that a medieval M.P. often wished that the votes of his electors had been bestowed elsewhere.

But now the times were changing. It was still no joyful task for M.P.s to return home at the end of the session with the tidings that they had agreed to a further dose of taxation. But there were other things to compensate for this unpleasant duty. Members, many of them elected under the high patronage of noblemen and statesmen, were being drawn to the capital, not only for the splendour of public life, but in search of office. For London was also the training ground for civil servants and statesmen. The queen could still talk of 'mysteries of state' outside the range and experience of the parliamentarians; but as the decades passed such talk carried less and less conviction. Government in England was becoming less of an autocracy and more of a partnership.

The English monarchy, for centuries, had not governed alone. It could not make laws without the agreement of the two Houses of Parliament. It could not impose direct taxation, or taxes on trade (other than certain traditional ones) without the same consent. But the political scene had largely been dominated by the king and the baronage, sometimes co-operating, but more often disputing among themselves. In these contests the knights of the shire and the burgesses of the towns, sitting in the lower house, could play no dominant part. Hence, they were generally glad to complete their exiguous business and go home. But, from about the middle of the sixteenth century, for reasons which are still being hotly debated among historians, the economic strength of those who sat in the lower house grew. It grew proportionately against that of the crown, and of the aristocracy also. With this accession to their economic strength there grew also a desire for influence in public affairs, including religion, diplomacy, trade and the marriage of the queen herself. But these things, she claimed, were 'matters of estate', they belonged to her high prerogative over which the Commons had no authority. She was prepared on occasion to listen graciously to their petitions, but she recognized no right in them to proceed by parliamentary bill.

Here then were the germs of deadlock in government. The queen could refuse the Commons a share in many aspects of policy, hold them in tutelage, decline to admit them to the mysteries of state. But they, in return, could tighten their grasp on their purse strings, and meet her large necessities with modest grants. Tenths and fifteenths, and subsidies—these were the main sources of direct taxation—were handicapped by traditional procedures and, in any case, trebly hard to obtain, from Parliament in the first stage, from the taxpayer in the second, and from the collector at the end. But the costs of government were mounting, while the non-parliamentary revenues—rents, feudal dues, ancient taxes upon trade—could in no way rise to fill the gap between income and commitments.

So it came about that the whole political life of England was beginning to be governed by an implied contract : namely, that the Commons would yield taxes provided that the queen's policy took regard of their needs. The Commons tried sometimes to ensure that the contract would be fully honoured. For example, when they were called upon to grant a subsidy in 1566, they inserted in the preamble to the bill a detailed statement of the queen's undertaking, that she would 'declare the succession . . . to the joyful comfort of us all'. She would have none of it. 'I know no reason,' she scrawled at the foot of their draft preamble, 'why any of my private answers to the realm should serve for prologue to a subsidies-book !' (There was indeed good reason : it was a desperate attempt to pin her down.)

'Is there no hold of'—reliance upon—'my speech without an act compel me to confirm?' (Unfortunately, in this case there was not.) 'If these fellows,' she concluded bitterly, 'were well answered, and paid with lawful coin, there would be fewer counterfeits among them.'

The preamble had to be changed. But the incident was a sign of the times. The Commons were trying to turn their grants into conditional grants; in essence, they were trying to gain control of policy. If they failed, then they would later on slow down the flow of money, go a long way towards sterilizing government, and wait for government to collapse—as it did under Charles I. One day, indeed, the Commons would wrest a large part of government from the monarchy and take it into their own hands. The queen did not live to see this revolution—for revolution it was—but both the struggle and the ultimate victory were in the background behind all the love-play between herself and her parliamentarians. The pressure upon her to marry was one indication of the shape of things to come. The religious issue was another.

In religion the queen had, in 1559, her first brush with the Commons—that is to say, the vigorous Protestant section of it—and had let them carry through far more than she originally intended. But the Commons thought that it was not enough : in particular, they lamented the lack of severity in punishing those who refused to take the Oath of Supremacy to the queen. In 1563 the same group resumed the struggle to purge the nation of all popish remains. The zealous

Dean Nowell who, in his sermon said some blunt things to the queen about her marriage, was even more blunt on the subject of the Catholics. His solution to the problem was characteristically simple : 'maintainers of false religion ought to die by the sword.' The Speaker of the House of Commons, describing Catholics as serpents, considered that their very survival was a grave reflection upon the faith of Englishmen. 'Having God's word and His name even in our mouths,' he cried, 'yet we live as infidels!'

These calls to their duty did not go unheard among the faithful. Indeed, ever on the watch, they saw in some bills the threat of a return to papistry, in others an opportunity for striking a further blow at the papists. Hence, when a bill to increase shipping was introduced, under which Wednesdays as well as Saturdays would become officially established fish days, it ran into dogged resistance because it too closely resembled the Catholic dietary laws. Even an affirmation in the statute that the fish days had nothing to do with any 'superstition' could not set troubled minds at rest.

But it was more especially in the new Supremacy Bill that the Protestant activists showed their teeth. The first Elizabethan Act of 1559 had required ecclesiastics and public officials to take the oath acknowledging the queen as Supreme Governor of the Church of England. Failure to do so meant suspension from office. To go further and maintain that the Bishop of Rome was head of the church meant imprisonment.

Harsh punishment, it might seem, but to some Members of Parliament, with their invasion neurosis, it did not seem harsh enough. In 1563 they extended the reach of the supremacy statute to take in many more sections of the community, including Members of Parliament, schoolmasters, lawyers and all university graduates. They also sharpened its claws. A refusal to take the oath, on the first occasion it was offered, carried the penalties of loss of all one's lands and property, in addition to imprisonment. On the second refusal it carried the death penalty of treason. Here indeed was the fulfilment of Dean Nowell's prayer that the maintainers of a false religion should be put to the sword! The queen had recoiled from too drastic a punishment in 1559. She did so again in 1563. But the pressure was too heavy and the law went through. Yet what looked like total victory for the extremists was neutralized by a supreme Elizabethan strategem. The death penalty came with the second refusal to take the oath. Very well; the queen directed her archbishop, Parker, that it was not to be administered a second time, without written instruction from her. In fact, such instruction never came. In this context, the direction applied to ecclesiastics. But what went for the church went for the state. Men were not executed in Elizabethan England simply for not taking the oath of supremacy.

This one incident exemplifies the whole pattern of the queen's policy, from the beginning to the end of her reign. She knew what it was, in her sister's day, to live in a glass house, ever visible to the prying eyes of the

inquisitors who would make a window into her soul.
Now that she was in power, she would not treat her
subjects in the same way, even though the pressure
upon her to do so was heavy. Many parliamentarians
believed that to allow Catholic dissidents to exist in
their midst was to gamble with their security, as the
queen was to gamble again, later on, when they pressed
her to execute Mary, Queen of Scots. Elizabeth believed, on the other hand, that to cut off a sincere
minority of her subjects, solely because of their religion,
was to throw away wantonly the unity of England. It
was perhaps fortunate for England at this time that her
ruler was one who apparently held no powerful and
intransigent views on religion. Three monarchs of
strong, and exclusive, religious views were succeeded by
a *politique*. It was as well.

The Commons would live on to fight these battles
with the queen, over religion and marriage, again and
again. But soon the problem of another queen's marriage, that of Mary, Queen of Scots, precipitated one of
the great crises of the reign. First there was inaugurated
a pantomime in which there were four principal
actors: Cecil, Dudley, De Quadra (the Spanish ambassador) and Elizabeth herself, although her appear-
ances on the stage were usually fleeting. She had the
more important roles of script-writer and stage-
manager, both of which involved a good deal of
improvisation. For it seemed at times as though the
queen had not yet completed writing their parts when
she put her actors on the stage, and that she watched

their performances—and Mary's improvisations—before deciding what they should do next. It seems also that Elizabeth was uncertain to the last as to what her own words would be as she rang down the curtain. In England the whole business of Elizabeth's marriage contained many elements of high comedy. In Scotland, the problem of Mary's marriage ended in high tragedy.

At the end of 1560, on the death of her husband, Francis II, Mary had found herself, at the age of 18, a widow and an ex-queen of France. The question of her next marriage was, to England, second in importance only to that of Elizabeth herself. And, second only to Elizabeth, she became the most sought-after lady in the British Isles. She was nine years Elizabeth's junior, a lively and attractive creature with her Scottish charm and volatile temperament. She was warm-hearted, high-spirited, romantic : welcome qualities in a woman, dangerous qualities in a queen, especially so in the dour capital of the north. 'In communication with her' wrote her life-long enemy, the Calvinist John Knox, 'I espied such craft as I have not found in such age.' But not enough craft, in any sense of the word. She was at once caught up in the knots of baronial intrigue, domestic religious discord and Anglo-Scottish diplomacy; and the knots were ultimately cut, not by statesmanship, but by the executioner's axe.

Soon Mary's marriage became a shuttlecock between the great powers. Don Carlos of Spain was one nominee for her hand, a proposal which was, in effect, vetoed

by the governments of England and France, neither
of whom—for their own reasons—was willing to see
a Franco-Scottish alliance give place to a Spanish-
Scottish one. The Hapsburg Archduke Charles was
brought forward and turned down, this time by the
Scottish leaders. Charles IX of France was suggested
but the proposal came to nothing. Robert Dudley himself, now decked out with the Earldom of Leicester,
was nominated by Elizabeth; and Mary—only with the
greatest effort—succeeded in making her refusal a
polite one. So in the end Mary resolved to take the
matter into her own hands and, to the consternation
of England, married Henry, Lord Darnley, without
tarrying for the blessings of Elizabeth or anyone else.

This was not the sudden emotional act that one
would expect from Mary, but a calculated decision.
For Darnley was, after Mary, next in succession to the
English throne. He was, moreover, born in England
and, in name at least, a Protestant. By the marriage
Mary boldly underwrote her own succession; and it
was indeed the son of this brief marriage who, nearly
forty years later, as James I ascended the English
throne. Darnley's good claim to the Tudor crown undoubtedly strengthened his suit with Mary. He also
had a good claim to the Scottish crown, after Mary;
but that was a deadly inheritance. For he inherited
also the bitter disputes of faction and the bloody affrays
which, for decades, were to soil the pages of Scottish
history. If by some miracle he had inherited (in addi-

tion to title) patience and statesmanship, he might by a hundredth chance have steered his wife and his country away from internecine warfare to the ultimately safe anchorage of the united throne of England and Scotland. Instead of these rare virtues, he was endowed with impatience, vanity and a crude and jealous temperament, which flared up finally into the murder of the queen's secretary, David Rizzio, believed by Darnley to be her lover.

This crime was carried out in the presence of the queen herself; and its effects were devastating. From now onwards any political skills she may have possessed deserted her, and she swung with emotion from one folly to another. Darnley expiated his murder of Rizzio by his own murder less than a year later; and in February 1567 Mary, now aged 25, found herself a widow for the second time. Worse even than that, she found her name, two days later, placarded in Edinburgh as the accomplice of James Hepburn, Earl of Bothwell, her husband's murderer.

Afterwards a box of letters was produced—famous from that day to this as the 'casket letters'—which, if they were genuine, established beyond doubt the guilt of Mary, apparently sending love letters to Bothwell shortly before the murder. But were they genuine? Or was Mary the victim of unscrupulous traducers who would go on blackening her name until the day she died? It has been a labyrinthine controversy which has wound its way tirelessly through the centuries and engaged the attentions and the reputations of investigators of all kinds. The arguments in favour of their being genuine probably outweigh those on the other side, though not by very much. But, in effect, far more damaging than the casket letters was Mary's conduct in this supreme crisis of her life. That she had endured much at the hands of her unspeakable husband, there can be no doubt. As a result, much could have been forgiven her, although hardly the fore-knowledge of her husband's murder. But to do now as she did and marry the known murderer of her husband (on the shallow pretext of her forcible seizure), seemed almost designed to alienate even the most devoted of her followers—or, at least, should have done had not Scotland been riven by warring factions. Some still clung to her but even this tough band of men, never very large, could not save her. In May 1568, utterly routed, she fled across the border, trusting to the assistance of her fellow monarch the Queen of England, and thirsting for revenge.

The contrast between Mary's behaviour at the time of her husband's murder and Elizabeth's behaviour at the time of Amy Robsart's death is so sharp that one sees it almost as an object-lesson for statesmen and historians. Certainly, the lesson was not lost on Elizabeth. She was bound, of course, to give Mary political asylum. But was she bound also to give Mary moral and military support in the well-nigh hopeless task of reconquering her kingdom?

If she did, Elizabeth would at once throw away her Scottish allies, who would be bound to turn elsewhere for their friends. By intervening on the wrong side Elizabeth would make Scotland safe—not for Mary—but for the French. On the other hand, to send Mary back to Scotland a captive would not only be an act wholly lacking in humanity but utterly alien to Elizabeth's conception of monarchy as something beyond the touch of the subject's hands. There was a third possibility open to Elizabeth and that was to wash her hands of the whole business: banish Mary from England and let her go where she pleased. But, it must be remembered, Mary was the claimant to the *English* as well as the Scottish throne. In a darkening European situation she might well be used as the spearhead for an invasion of this country from the continent. It may be, as has been suggested, that the reverse would have happened, that a thoroughly discredited Mary would have blunted any projects on her behalf. But for so sophisticated an argument there were, at the time, no grounds whatsoever; and Elizabeth quite rightly declined to take any risks.

Elizabeth decided to keep Mary in England as an involuntary guest—in effect a prisoner—simply because she felt that she could not let her go. It was a difficult decision to take, for Elizabeth was harbouring an inveterate enemy whose ambitions would grow by the false hopes they fed upon. Here was a problem to which Elizabeth never found a solution and, in the end, her ministers virtually took the decision out of her hands. In the long years which followed, Mary must have often regretted her catastrophic entanglements first with Darnley, then with Bothwell. So, undoubtedly, did Elizabeth.

Chapter Five

A Time for Decision, 1568–72

'TELL the [Spanish] ambassador', wrote Mary, Queen of Scots, at the beginning of 1569, 'that if his master will help me, I shall be Queen of England in three months, and Mass shall be said all over the country.' In the event, the King of Spain did not help Mary; and, if Mass was said in England, it was only in the secret recesses of private houses or in embassy chapels. But although, for the present, Mary pleaded for help in vain, her message in fact contained the essence of the unfolding diplomatic scene. In 1568 it would still have been impossible to draw firmly the future pattern of international relations. By 1572 the pattern was quite clear and, as long as Elizabeth lived, it would not change. Western Europe and the open seas would, from now on, provide the multi-coloured background against which Elizabeth and Philip II of Spain would strive for mastery. By the time the old king died, in 1598, it would be manifest that, although England's supremacy still lay in the future, the age of Spanish preponderance in Europe was drawing to a close.

But however optimistic the letters of the Scottish queen, Philip II was never the man to involve himself in an open struggle with England merely to pull Mary's chestnuts out of the fire. If he intervened, it would be because Spanish interests were at stake. He might come in also because *Catholic* interests were at stake, but here his role was somewhat ambiguous. It is not wholly un-just to his memory to assert that, if Spanish and Catho-lic interests conflicted, Philip made what must have been, for him, the unhappy choice of his nation and his dynasty as against his church. Hence his extraordinary position as protector of Elizabeth at a time when the Vatican was preaching fire and sword against her. Throughout his long life Philip was bombarded with the letters of English *emigrés*, who gave him a picture of a country seething with discontent and ready to rise at the first sound of a Spanish gun in the English channel. Philip read their missives, annotated them, circulated them through the endless corridors of the Spanish civil service and then, in most cases, did nothing about them. It is true that the Spanish embassy in London gave comfort and help to a whole procession of intriguers and traitors against the queen; and, had domestic rebellions looked like succeeding, Philip, of course, would have taken a hand in the proceedings. But he would not hazard an invasion army upon the speculations of gamblers and the dreams of idealists. When at last the Armada did sail, it was a sign that, for Philip, all other hope of a settlement with Elizabeth had passed away.

For the Spanish king and the English queen had much more in common than emerges from a brief ex-amination of their policies. If we set aside their utterly contrasting attitudes to religion, and some of their utterances designed for domestic consumption, we are at once struck by how much they shared : a cautious and tortuous diplomacy, a reluctance to come to irrevocable decisions, a close personal grasp upon power, and—each in his own way—a loving and unremitting service of his country. But if the queen's task was difficult, the king's was impossible.

To a monarch of Philip's temper, it was hardly likely that a letter from Mary, Queen of Scots, would act as a clarion call to war. But there were other pressures upon him; and events which occurred in the English channel and on the other side of the Atlantic, at about the same time as Mary's letter, underlined for Philip the fundamental question of peace or war. It placed exactly the same issue before Elizabeth. Upon her answer to it would depend the future greatness of England. For she must now decide whether she should encourage and sustain her bolder spirits, eager to take advantage of the geographical revolution which the century was witnessing; or whether, if she could, she should damp their ardours and reject the great—and hazardous—opportunity opening before their eyes.

Since the end of the fifteenth century, part of the new world across the Atlantic had been known and annexed. The same was true of West Africa. But nearly all the limitless tracts of both continents were barred to England by the Treaty of Tordesillas of 1494, under which Spain and Portugal, by authority of papal bull, shared most of these continents between them, Spain taking the greater part of America, and Portugal taking the rest and Africa as well. As the years passed this position became increasingly untenable. In a rare moment of frankness, William Cecil had once told the Spanish ambassador that the pope 'had no right to partition the world and to give and take kingdoms to whomever he pleased'. In this, at least, Cecil spoke for the generality. English seamen could not, and would not, be confined to the narrow seas and the coastal waters of Europe. For them, England was no longer an insignificant island lying to the north-west of the European continent, on the perimeter of the main currents of trade. For them, England was the hinge of the door as it swung open from the old world to the new.

John Hawkins of Plymouth was the pioneer of the new outlook; and the queen backed him. The Spanish colonists of the new world were crying out for labour which the native population was quite inadequate to supply. Labour they had been getting in the shape of negro slaves, bought or captured on the African coast and transported by traders across the Atlantic. But the Spaniards had not so far had negro slaves through the good offices of the English; and it was the peculiar mission of Hawkins, in 1562, to add an English link to this promising chain. By so intervening he performed the double feat of infringing Portuguese rights in Africa and Spanish rights in America; but he delivered the goods, and he was welcome. The business was also profitable. So, when he came again, he was backed by the queen and her ministers, who sank money in his project; and this too showed a profit. So he came a third time. But now the politicians had to be reckoned with. In September 1568 Hawkins, with his fleet of armed trading vessels, lay in the port of San Juan de Ulua, in the gulf of Mexico. Here too came the Spanish squadron, with the Viceroy, Enriquez, on board. For a time relations between the two fleets seemed friendly enough. Then, without warning, the Spaniard struck with brutal treachery. When the smoke died away, Hawkins dragged himself home, as did only one other ship, captained by his cousin, Sir Francis Drake. In January and February 1569, after great hardships, they reached home waters, with memories that would scorch for decades through the diplomatic relations of England and Spain.

Hawkins was no innocent seaman engaged in the friendly commerce of peace. To get his negro slaves he had to fight for some of them in Africa. To persuade some Spaniards in America to purchase his precious cargo he had burnt down part of a town and looted its treasure. Yet he was no pirate, in the ordinary sense of the word, although the Spaniards hanged members of his crew when they could lay hands on them. But it was, in any case, becoming impossible to engage in peaceful trading with Spanish possessions overseas. Philip, if he could, would take a stranglehold upon the whole of his communications, even if it choked his own colonies in the process. So English seamen were forced to turn to a kind of political piracy against him, whether they liked it or not. They liked it.

Political piracy is what Elizabeth herself indulged in. At the time when news of San Juan de Ulua was coming through, she was herself engaged, in the English channel, in violating the conventions of peaceful trade. But this was a security measure of national importance, involving ultimately the independence of both this country and the Netherlands.

For the year 1568 saw the destinies of these two small countries linked together in a bitter and long-drawn-out struggle with Spain. The seventeen provinces of the Netherlands were linked also to Philip II, but that was merely by dynastic marriage, the result of the family policies of the Hapsburgs. The people of the Low Countries and Spain were bound neither by race nor economic interest; while the coming of Calvinism intensified the differences already existing. This was especially true of the northern provinces bordering on the sea. Since Philip's accession they had tried, by one means or another, to safeguard their old liberties and gain some new ones. Led by William of Orange and Count Egmont, they had been prepared to maintain the Spanish connection, but only if their liberties were secure. They were not; and the execution of Egmont and his colleague Hoorn in 1568 broke the last thread of hope joining the Dutch with their Spanish masters. Philip II for his part decided that he had no alternative but to hold down his recalcitrant provinces by force. Under the Duke of Alva, the full weight of Spanish repression descended upon the Dutch; and it looked as though those unfortunate people who still resisted must be flung into the sea.

But, as has happened time and time again in our own history, the sea was their saviour, and the Dutch 'sea beggars' as they came to be known,—a title at first derisively given and then proudly assumed—pursued their own brand of naval warfare against Philip. An imperial policy of repression is, moreover, always more expensive than one of conciliation, both in blood and treasure—especially treasure. And, for the Spaniards, treasure was far to seek. In 1568 they acquired a considerable quantity in Italy on loan, for the use of Alva. The fleet carrying it was chased by pirates—French ones this time—and sought refuge in southern English ports. Elizabeth seized the silver, claiming by a somewhat imperfect logic that, since Philip had merely borrowed the money, it was not yet his and she was therefore entitled to transfer the money to herself.

It is, of course, impossible to offer any legal defence for an action of this sort, second-cousin as it was to piracy. But, within the context of power politics, in which Elizabeth was already a skilled practitioner, she could easily justify the step she took. The money was undoubtedly to be used to stamp out Dutch resistance. Once that was accomplished, there could be no doubt that Alva's victorious armies would be free to seek a foothold across the narrow channel, to bring peace and conformity to England, lair of pirates and breeding ground of Protestants. If, when the queen seized the Italian loan, she may have already known about the recent attack upon her ships in colonial waters, she was also fully conscious of the dangers nearer home.

The Italian lenders were perfectly happy to accept the *fait accompli* : Elizabeth's credit was better than Philip's. London was a safe harbour for the money as compared with the pirate-infested English channel or the Netherlands sieve through which Spanish wealth was fast draining away. To the Netherlanders, hanging on grimly to their last strip of land, it was a magnificent gesture; especially as there was no question yet of an alliance between England and the Dutch. But if the seizure of the loan was not the warlike act of an ally, it was a wonderful piece of co-belligerency; and the Netherlanders recognized it as such.

It was also identified in that way by the Spaniards who, in their fury, let loose counter-measures against the English in the Low Countries. They cut England's main artery of trade through Antwerp and hastened— but did not cause—a shift in the direction of English commerce. As the year 1568 ended, it looked as though England and Spain were on the eve of war. But Philip, like Elizabeth, paused at the brink, and was glad to turn away.

Here was one more example of how much these two rulers had in common, although their approach was hardly shared by their more vocal subjects, or by their brother monarchs in Europe. We think of Philip II as master of the greatest of empires and of Elizabeth as the inspiration of a small, but virile and expansionist, nation; all of which serves to obscure the fact that they were both *conservative* statesmen, concerned above all to retain what they held rather than to blaze a trail of adventure. During these years both Philip's and Elizabeth's capacity to restrain their own hotheads was strained to the uttermost. But such caution as both rulers displayed did not preclude their subjects from the time-honoured sport of fishing in each other's troubled waters. It is true that some of the fishermen might be wrecked in the storm; but, if they were not, there were some enormous fish to land.

The Dutch Netherlands, the most northerly provinces of Spain, gave Philip the greatest trouble, differing as they did from Spain in religion as well as economic and social structure. That same contrast was to be seen between the northern counties of England and the queen's government in London. To the Queen of England (as were his to the King of Spain) her northerly provinces were, at this time, a thorn in her flesh. They were troublesome, dissident, distrustful, smouldering with a score of discontents. But there was one important contrast between the border counties of northern England and the Netherlands provinces of Spain. For the Netherlands represented the most advanced ideas in commerce and civilization, while northern England still lagged far behind the outlook and practices of the much more progressive south.

For that very reason the enemies of Elizabeth probed deeply into the backward, sparsely populated regions of the north, and nourished the discontents of their aristocratic leaders, like the Earls of Northumberland

and Westmorland. To such men it seemed that the traditions and long-established religion of England were being betrayed by a southern clique of smooth, upstart politicians, led by Cecil, who were thrusting their new-fangled Protestantism upon an unwilling nation. Certain counsellors, they said, have 'crept in about the Prince . . . excluded the nobility from the Prince'—long ago, at the time of the Pilgrimage of Grace of 1536 the northern rebels had said the same thing of Thomas Cromwell and his colleagues—'and had set such law contrary to the honour of God and the wealth [welfare] of the realm'.

These discontents were easily fed by De Spes, the Spanish ambassador in London, who performed the double service of exaggerating to the earls the amount of support they could expect from Philip, and exaggerating to Philip the strength behind the northern earls. Philip had been too long in the business of governing to pay much attention to the sanguine imagination of his ambassador; but the northern earls were less experienced and they did not tarry for either wisdom or Philip II.

Had this sorry affair been the work simply of a couple of backwoods peers and an indiscreet ambassador, the whole thing could have been nipped pretty speedily in the bud. But English discord at this time had some of the attributes of a fugue, with its elaborate point counter-point, plot woven into plot, until half the courts of Europe were drawn in, as well as the counter-espionage service of Elizabeth's government.

The northern earls, in one sense, operated on the fringe of the main plot, which had its centre further south in the person of Mary, Queen of Scots. With her union to Bothwell about to be dissolved, she was now the candidate for a fourth husband, by means of whom she hoped to gain a protector, the throne of Scotland—and perhaps more than that. By 1569 her name was being closely linked with that of the Duke of Norfolk, head of the powerful Howard family and the only duke in the kingdom. The exact conditions of the proposed marriage bargain we do not know; but in effect it meant nothing less than an attempt to divert power from Cecil, and perhaps from Elizabeth herself, to the Mary-Howard faction, a faction which drew its support from a large section of the community including—for a time—some of Elizabeth's own ministers. She recognized the situation for the grave threat it presented and solemnly warned Norfolk of the dangerous game he was playing.

Norfolk—never a strong personality—hastened to disclaim all share in the manoeuvre; but, as the plot started to crumble, the northern earls felt that they must act at once, or else abandon all hope. In other words, the rebels took action sooner than they should. The result, after some initial and illusory successes, was a *débâcle*.

By breaking the plot up into its component parts, the Elizabethan government broke the plot itself. It was especially fortunate that one element in it, papal intervention, was thereby forced badly out of time.

Pope Pius V was, of course, no plotter. In many ways a great idealist, he was appalled that the politically minded rulers of Europe could, for more than a decade, live cheek by jowl with the shameless champion of protestant heresy. He could, no doubt, see that, in his own time and for his own reasons, the French or Spanish king would bring his army to bear upon Elizabeth. But Pius was deeply conscious also that his own predecessors as pope had too often sullied the high ideals of their church with material and tactical considerations. He was cast in a different mould, and he resolved to strike at once with the sword of the spirit, even though the secular swords rusted in the scabbards of the self-styled defenders of Christendom.

But Pius V was not wholly blind to the political opportunities at hand; his bull of excommunication and deposition was timed to inspire—or crown—the heroic achievements of the northern rebels. Unfortunately for his timing, while he was putting his finishing touches to his bull, in February 1570, the routed followers of the northern earls were already hanging from their gibbets in the villages of the border country. When, at last, one bold spirit dared to fasten his bull to the door of the Bishop of London, in May 1570, it it was already discredited by the events of the preceding winter.

Philip II of Spain could read the political signs clearly enough; but his ambassador in London could not. Nor could a certain Roberto Ridolphi, a Florentine banker who deserted international finance for international plotting, with disastrous results for those who shared his fantasies. But many did not share them. And when, for example, some of the details of the plot were passed on to Elizabeth by—of all people—the Grand Duke of Tuscany, she was fully ready for it. Norfolk had allowed himself, for the second time, to become involved in the Marian marriage scheme, but on this occasion he was not pardoned. Still, Elizabeth long hesitated in punishing him, from January 1572 when the death sentence was passed until the following June, when she assented to his execution. Her ministers believed that national security required the execution of Norfolk; but here they ran into the resistance of the queen. As always, her sense of duty triumphed; but the emotional cost to her of this victory lies outside the normal measuring scale of the historian.

There is a footnote to the Ridolphi plot and its unhappy end for Norfolk. When, in January 1572, he believed that he faced execution, he wrote a humble submission to the queen which, in spite of its grovelling language, has a tragic dignity about it. He could not ask for pardon—that was out of the question—but he asked forgiveness, and he coupled with it a plea for his orphan children, already without a mother and shortly to be deprived of a father. His plea was that 'My carrion end may take away and assuage so Your Majesty's just ire as that the little poor wretches may taste of Your Highness's great clemency'. The clemency he sought was that they should be given into the guard-

ianship of William Cecil (created Baron Burghley in
1571). Here is one of the many paradoxes of Elizabethan society. The Ridolphi plot, with Norfolk as its
active partisan, had been aimed at destroying Burghley. It misfired and destroyed Norfolk. Yet Norfolk's
prayer, as he prepared to leave this world, was that his
children should be committed to his late enemy 'for the
old love, goodwill and friendship that he hath borne to
me, their woeful father'.

This letter was written on January 21, 1572. Two
days later Norfolk wrote again to the queen, expressing
his deep gratitude for her agreement to this proposal
for 'my poor unfortunate brats which now, in their
shipwreck, be cast into the fearful surges of the sea'.
The following month he gave his final instructions
about the upbringing of his children and the disposal of
his property. He asked that his daughters 'Nan and
May might continue together. So likewise my three sons,
till years alter the course of their life. And if it might be,
that Moll and little Bess were also kept together.' But
all this was governed by a general direction : 'Nothing
to be done, neither by my children nor servants, without my Lord Burghley's privity.'

By the middle of 1572, Norfolk was dead and the
Ridolphi plot had gone the way of the Northern Rising.
The papal bull had fallen short of its target. For the
time being, also, England enjoyed the friendship of
France, where the Protestant Huguenot party under
Coligny held its brief dominion. In Madrid, it
is true, there was still talk of how to murder the English

queen; but Alva, Philip's viceroy in the Netherlands, was urging upon his master a policy of negotiation, not invasion. Still, it would have been an utter illusion if Elizabeth's government had, at this stage, believed itself to be secure, or the papal bull of no political significance.

On the contrary, it treated the papal bull as the gravest of threats. 'This very woman,' the bull had said, 'having seized the kingdom and monstrously usurped the place of Supreme Head of the Church in all England and the chief authority and jurisdiction thereof, hath again reduced the said kingdom into a miserable and ruinous condition.' Accordingly, the pope continued, 'We do declare her to be deprived of her pretended title to the kingdom aforesaid, and of all dominion, dignity, and privilege whatsoever; and also the nobility, subjects, and people of the said kingdom, and all others who have in any sort sworn unto her, to be for ever absolved from any such oath, and all manner of duty of dominion, allegiance and obedience.' No wonder, 'the pretended Queen of England, the servant of wickedness,' looked to her defences.

Elizabeth wanted no panic measures. But every Protestant in England knew how much depended on the preservation of the queen's life. She was, said one M.P., 'not only, in respect of our goods and lives, the singular stay, but for truth and religion, yea of all Christendom, not simply the *great,* but in this world the *sole,* hope'.[1] As ever in an attack on the Catholics, the parliamentar-

[1] I have translated the italicized words from the original Latin.

ians wanted to go much further than the queen. She agreed that they should declare invalid the title of anyone who claimed the throne during Elizabeth's lifetime —in other words, Mary, Queen of Scots. This was reasonable enough. But they would have gone further and extended the ban to that person's heirs; and it was here that they ran into the solid resistance of Elizabeth. Yet, if they could not have it all their own way, they succeeded in putting through some very powerful legislation in the Parliament of 1571. To seek the overthrow of the queen, to declare that she was not entitled to the throne, or to describe her as a heretic or schismatic was henceforth to be high treason. To publish papal bulls in this country equally brought the full penalty of high treason.

By these measures, the queen's government and Parliament acknowledged the conditions of ideological warfare. For they not only had the papal bull to contend with, but the beginnings of a great English missionary movement, taking its source at Douai in 1568 and spreading from there to other European cities. With such centres springing up on the continent, some of the best men among the younger generation were being attracted abroad to the profound and rigorous training of the missionary priesthood, to be followed by a return to England to the noble service of its re-conversion and, ultimately, to the beatific joys of martyrdom. Henceforth, Elizabeth would be faced, not simply with an old guard of Catholicism in England, holding together the decaying fragments of an ancient church, but with a

renewed, inspired movement, an army of young idealists, English to the core, yet radiant with the new dawn
of Rome. They had no political objectives, and were,
indeed, forbidden to take part in political discussion.
But they were also instructed to help restore in England
a faith prohibited by English law, a church whose head
had declared that the English queen was a usurping
tyrant and had placed under anathema all who obeyed
her rule. With this exacting dilemma before them, the
Catholic missionaries sought heroically for a way of
serving God yet witholding nothing from their tribute
to Caesar.

Elizabeth's government refused to believe that this
dilemma could be resolved, that these young men were
anything but a front for the political aspirations of the
pope and the secular monarchs supporting him. Moreover, from all over England came increasing evidence of
dangerous dissent; and from Europe signs that the pope
and his allies would strike at Elizabeth where opportunity served.

It was not in Elizabeth's nature to meet a political
crisis with purely political weapons. So, in a darkening
situation, she renewed her faith in an old and familiar
trick of hers: she would offer her hand in marriage.
This time her fancy lighted upon the brother of Charles
IX of France, the nineteen-year-old Duke of Anjou,
destined himself one day to rule France as Henry III,
her last Valois king. The proposal of marriage was first
aired during the autumn of 1570, at a time when
Catharine de Medici, Queen-Mother of France, was

seeking to counter-balance the encroaching power of
the Catholics at home and of Philip II of Spain. Anjou,
as it happened, was also a strong candidate for the hand
of Mary, Queen of Scots, a fact which perhaps lent a
little fervour to Elizabeth's own suit. None the less, its
primary object was to buy for England a major European ally.

But Elizabeth had cried Wolf! before and—now
aged 37—enjoyed a considerable reputation for ambiguous matrimonial ventures. Hence Catharine's acid
remark that, if the Queen of England had a daughter,
she would be more appropriate for a marriage with the
young duke. Far more serious as an impediment to
marriage than the disparity of age was the disparity of
religion. In the eyes of even his own mother, Anjou was
not simply a faithful Catholic, but a fanatical one. He
heard, she said, three or four Masses a day, and fasted
so devoutly in Lent that his health was threatened. She
almost wished that he were a Huguenot rather than a
Catholic. On the other hand, according to a foreign
observer, he was 'completely dominated by voluptuous-
ness'. He had a passion for perfume, jewellery, clothes
and the ladies of the court. A fanatic, a fop and a
voluptuary : a somewhat difficult consort for the cold
Queen of England.

Elizabeth's own ministers were not sure whether her
intentions were serious or not; but, meanwhile, the
representatives of the two countries pressed on with the
suit right through 1571 and into 1572. Sir Thomas
Smith, Elizabeth's ambassador and a shrewd judge of

the times, was sent to France to find some compromise with Anjou; and it was then, at the beginning of 1572, that the whole scheme collapsed on the rocks of religious intolerance. Elizabeth, he reported to Catharine, was willing to go a long way to help Anjou, and would indeed grant him the full private exercise of his religion. But this, replied Catharine, was not enough : he demanded its full *public* exercise as well. At this, even the diplomatic Smith was shaken off his balance. 'Then,' he cried aghast, 'he may require also the four orders of friars, monks, canons, pilgrimages, pardons, oil, cream, relics and all such trumperies.' That undoubtedly, was the end of the match. But it was not the end of the negotiations between the two queens.

In place of the unyielding Anjou, Catharine offered his younger brother, the more flexible Duke of Alençon, closely identified with the French Protestants. This may have seemed at the time no more than the absurd anticlimax to a charade of diplomatic nonsense; but, in the event, Alençon's suit came nearer to success than did that of any other candidate (with the possible exception of Leicester) for the hand of Elizabeth. But, suddenly, while the two queens were examining the possibilities of such a match, the brief friendship between England and France was rudely shattered by the alarming news from Paris of the events of St Bartholomew's Day, 1572. In the space of twenty-four hours, three or four thousand Huguenots who had gathered in Paris were massacred and, from the capital, the bloodbath spread to the provinces, where thousands more met the same fate. Whether this ghastly vengeance was planned from the start by Catharine de Medici or—more likely—was the mismanagement of a political murder, followed by failure of nerve, it is hard to say. More important than what caused these events was what they were taken to mean in divided Europe. To the new pope, Gregory XIII, they were heavenly inspired acts, to be celebrated with a *Te Deum* at St Peter's. To Catholics like Philip II they symbolized the end of the French ruler's dalliance with the hated Protestants. To Elizabeth and her ministers they came as a clear warning of what the papal bull would bring to a divided England.

In the high summer of 1572, England seemed in grave peril. Yet the times had about them the stimulus and exhilaration of another summer, centuries later, when, as its greatest statesman told the nation, it had to be ready to hold out, *if necessary for years, if necessary alone.* Elizabeth was alone. She had been branded by the pope, and her subjects were thereby absolved from obedience to her. Her murder would, no doubt, be celebrated with the same piety that had greeted the massacre of the Huguenots. But she, and the majority of the nation, shared the peril and the mood of the hour. Perhaps the best expression of that mood came from the Recorder of the small town of Warwick, situated as it was at the very heart of England. In her reign he saw : 'The restoration of God's true religion, the speedy change of wars into peace, of dearth and famine into plenty, of an huge mass of dross and counterfeit money into fine gold and silver.' This, he affirmed, was 'to Your Highness's great honour, whose prosperous reign hitherto hath not been touched with any troublous season, the rude blast of one insurrection except'—that was the Rising of the Northern Earls. But that was 'soon blown over and appeased by God's favour and Your Majesty's wisdom'. The result was to make 'your happy government to shine more gloriously, even as the sun after dark clouds appeareth more clear and beautiful'.

Chapter Six

Ireland, the Netherlands and Spain, 1573–80

THE developing situation of the 1570s, as it presented itself to Elizabeth I, offered all the prospects of religious warfare. Some of her ministers, like Sir Francis Walsingham—and many of her Puritan subjects—would have been glad to join issue on those terms: to attack the Spaniard abroad because he was a Catholic, and to attack the Catholic at home because he might be used by the Spaniard. Yet Elizabeth herself refused to accept the situation in those terms.

She refused to be caught in an ideological trap, in which she would have to fight for principles irrespective of national interests. In this she revealed herself as far more realistic than many of her critics. She was empirical, they were theoretical. She showed a better grasp than did they upon political—and historical—factors. For, when all is said, nations do not usually fight for ideals alone, without regard to national interests. There are indeed dramatic exceptions; but a great nation could not long survive as a force to be reckoned with if it were easily blown into an untenable position by the wildest winds of irresponsible enthusiasms. It does often happen that ideals and national interests march together, or appear to; but it is not often that ideals alone inaugurate the war, although they may elevate and inspire the warring nations.

For Elizabeth it was a hard and thankless task to stand firm against her own idealists, to hold back when others said strike! It looked like lethargy, vacillation, lack of faith in the whole system upon which her monarchy was founded. Yet it was she, not the vigorous Protestant group, who was faithful to the interests of the monarchy and the unity of the nation. Henry VII had sought to give his monarchy a broad political base. So even had Henry VIII, in his own peculiar way; for, in spite of the damage he did to the fabric of Tudor society by carrying through the Reformation, he tried to embrace as much as he could of the traditional Church; (but he struck barbarously at the idealists and the extremists). Edward VI and Mary broke from the tradition by building their religious settlements on too narrow a sector of the community. Now Elizabeth tried to return to the earlier principle at the very time when it was hardest to apply. To let loose a holy war against her dissident subjects might have appeared as an example of a noble devotion to the cause of Protestantism: it would, in fact, have been to follow the line of least resistance. Worse still, it would have ended her hopes of national unity. In Elizabeth alone rested the ultimate power of decision; and, from her lonely position of eminence, she found it harder each year to pursue a policy which was as unpopular as it was moderate.

The policy bore also a second stigma, quite apart from appearing too tender to Catholic consciences. It seemed to come down with a particularly heavy hand upon the most Protestant of her subjects. For by now the Puritans were a force to be reckoned with.

The exact origin of the word 'Puritan' is somewhat obscure. It was being used in the 1560s in France and a decade later in England, where it meant one who wished to purify the Church from the impure, Roman practices which—it was claimed—were smothering it. The beginnings of Puritanism in this country may be seen in the Protestant activists of the early days of Elizabeth's reign, who could not understand why she tarried so long before establishing God's kingdom on earth. For the nature of that kingdom was clearly set out in the bible, the only infallible authority known to Puritans. The fact that the queen looked to other traditions, including that of her father and even her sister, showed either perversity or ignorance, which could only be remedied by instruction. As for the traditional vestments and ceremonials, the Puritan test was again simple enough. Were they to be found in the bible? As it happened, they were not. So it became necessary for the Puritans to prepare the queen for her long course of instruction; but from it, one must admit, they rather than she emerged the wiser.

The Puritans attacked the prayer book, the ecclesiastical formalities and some doctrines; and when Elizabeth told the bishops to enforce the older principles, they attacked the bishops as well (for whom, incidentally, the Puritans could find no justification in the bible either). From the first decade of Elizabeth's reign the Puritans made a two-pronged assault upon her Church settlement: in the ecclesiastical assembly of Convocation and in Parliament. In both spheres they were thwarted: the assault broke against the constitutional machinery and entrenched conservatism which still exercised power in Church and State; but it left scars behind. Also, when a radical movement fails before the defences of the existing order, the movement begins to undergo an organic change. The more lukewarm of its members tend to drift away and, in time, accept the doctrines of the establishment. Some, indeed, are ultimately found amongst the most formidable defenders of the institutions they once attacked. But a minority of the radical movement remain loyal to its creed and, as they run into unyielding opposition, grow more vigorous and intransigent in expounding their faith.

So it was with the Puritans. When it first began to take root, their movement counted among its supporters some of the great names in the Elizabethan church, including Parker, Elizabeth's first Archbishop of Canterbury, and Grindal, her second. Indeed, quite a number of Elizabeth's first bishops had, during their exile in Mary's reign, moved into a ready acceptance of the ideas of the continental reformers, Luther, Calvin or Zwingli. Now some of them found it difficult to adapt themselves to the Anglican order, steeped as it was in Roman forms. 'I confess', said one of her bishops, 'we suffer many things against our hearts, but we

cannot take them away . . . and we can innovate
nothing without the queen. Nor can we alter the laws.
The only thing left to our choice is whether we will
bear these things or break the peace of the Church.'
They bore these things.

The passing years, and the responsibilities of office,
further diluted the early ardours of the Church leaders,
and they became gradually more content with the
modest Protestantism of the English settlement. To
their more aggressive followers this looked like nothing
short of a gross betrayal, and they directed against the
bishops—instruments as they were of the queen's policy
of uniformity—the kind of venom especially reserved
for the lost leaders of reform. One diatribe, for example,
politely called a 'View of Antichrist, his laws and ceremonies in our English Church unreformed', showed
how closely the Pope of Lambeth conformed to the
practices of the Pope of Rome, and went on to list a
hundred examples of popery 'which deform the English
Reformation'.

The critics had taken up their positions before a
dozen years of Elizabeth's reign were over; but they
still had plenty of room to move, and still felt themselves to be members of the same Church. In the
'seventies, as new leaders emerged, the divisions hardened and the opposing sides found themselves taking
up situations from which they could not easily withdraw. Such hostility as already existed was now further
stiffened by theory as the rigorous doctrinal discipline
of Calvin took on its English texture in the writings of

Thomas Cartwright, appointed Lady Margaret Professor of Divinity at Cambridge in 1569 (and dismissed from that post in 1570). In his brilliant dialectic he forcefully expounded the Presbyterian doctrine that the true religious ministry consisted of equal men, whose authority derived from the bible and who acknowledged no superior in the Church but God. In such a system there was no call for the bishops, nor—if the argument was taken to its logical conclusion—for the queen herself. In the last analysis, Puritanism was a revolutionary movement in the Church; and—as the seventeenth century was to show—a revolution which began with the Church threatened the state.

The donnish Cartwright was not directly concerned with this, but many of his fellows were; at least they seized upon the essential point that a reformation which had been made in Parliament could also be unmade and remade in Parliament. Hence their claim to action in Parliament no less than in Convocation. That thesis the queen had encountered at the beginning of her reign and, in the 1559 Parliament, had compromised with it. But now she saw that the objectives of the Puritans were almost unlimited, and she thwarted them by every means she had to hand : censorship, eviction from ecclesiastical office, imprisonment. So the Puritans joined battle and, in the two Admonitions to Parliament of 1571 and 1572, put the issue squarely before the nation. The official prayer book, ordained to be used in all churches, was dismissed as 'an unperfect book, culled and picked out of the popish dunghill'. All right-thinking people were enjoined to 'remove homilies, articles, injunctions and that prescript order of service made out of the mass-book'. They were urged to 'take away the lordship, the loitering, the pomp, the idleness and livings of bishops'. The admonitions were, of course, never presented to Parliament. They were anonymous pamphlets, manifestoes of an aggressive body of resolute men who had mastered the techniques of propaganda. They were the opening volleys of a bitter party warfare.

As such the queen recognized them. She considered them, in one sense, more dangerous than the guided missiles of a distant pope. For the Puritans had a firm foothold in both Church and Parliament; they spoke, not in the rotund Latin of the papal curia, but in the authentic English accents of the pulpit and the market-place. If the queen could claim to be 'mere English', so could they.

They possessed also other weapons with which to fight their righteous cause. For, at the same time as their admonitions were directed to the people, over the heads of the bishops—and of the queen herself—the Puritans of south-east England were also busy strengthening the souls of the faithful by what were called 'exercises'—organized self-criticism by the ministers at periodic meetings, to which the laity also could be invited. The laudable aim of raising the spiritual and educational standards of the clergy—pitifully low at that time—was at first approved by the Church. But by 1577 Elizabeth had made her own assessment of these organizations, namely as dissident cells operating within the Church, in preparation for the day when the republic of God would be established. The republic did indeed come for a short time, during the 1650s, long after the queen was dead, with results which are well known. The first visions of the republic, as vouchsafed to the queen by her Puritans, were so repellent to her that she felt that the best way to postpone its coming was to stamp hard on the 'exercises'. She accordingly instructed Grindal (who had succeeded Parker as Archbishop of Canterbury in 1575) to suppress them. This, the archbishop politely replied, he could not agree to do —an indication to what high places some aspects of Puritanism had reached—and he was promptly suspended from office.

But not only could the Puritan spirit still be found on the bench of bishops. It was also active in the queen's council itself. Walsingham was known for his strong Puritan views. Leicester flirted with the movement from time to time. Even Burghley was thought to be sympathetic to it. But the queen stood fast and, in 1583, she found in Whitgift an archbishop after her own heart. Then there was formed a staunch alliance between churchman and queen against which the Puritan forces beat again and again without success. This is not to say that the queen solved the Puritan problem. Rather, as in other fields, she damped down the fires of opposition—and left them smouldering to her successor.

At the very time when the queen was trying to put

the 'exercises' under the ban she was, in the House of Commons, running into even more spirited opposition, personified from 1576 onwards in that inspired and heroic bigot, Peter Wentworth. Here was a man who loved Christianity passionately but believed that his own version of it had the unique virtues of truth; who informed the Archbishop of Canterbury to his face that he was merely aping the pope; who devoutly respected the queen yet told an astounded House of Commons that 'None is without fault; no, not our noble queen', and then went on to list her faults.

Here, in one man, was the clear link between religion and politics, the plain sign that the attack on the bishops could not stop short of the queen. 'It is a dangerous thing in a Prince,' cried Wentworth, 'unkindly to intreat and abuse his or her nobility and people, as Her Majesty did the last Parliament. And it is a dangerous thing in a Prince to oppose or bend herself against her nobility and people, yea against most loving and faithful nobility and people. And how could any Prince more unkindly intreat, abuse and oppose herself against her nobility and people than Her Majesty did the last Parliament?'

That Peter Wentworth loved liberty is beyond dispute. His famous sentence : 'Sweet indeed is the name of liberty and the thing itself a value beyond all inestimable treasure' is a sword-thrust through the sham of his day and ours. This Don Quixote of Elizabethan politics was in and out of prison in the latter part of his life—and died there—because he chose to speak his mind.

But the liberty he sought was, in the end, liberty for his minority faction to dictate the religion and the way of life of the whole nation. In those countries where it is not in power, a minority sometimes demands liberty of speech at the very time when its brothers-in-arms, already in control abroad, ruthlessly extinguish the last hopes of liberty. What the Puritans did when in power in Geneva under Calvin, and in England during the middle of the seventeenth century, taints the high zeal for liberty of men like Peter Wentworth. For, although he nobly suffered for liberty, he would never have extended that liberty to those who deviated from his own intolerant creed. No one can deny that, in defending and extending freedom of speech in the House of Commons, he won for himself an imperishable place in the history of democratic institutions. But the situation has its ironies. For, in thwarting Wentworth and the Puritans in these early battles, Elizabeth herself struck for liberty also: the ultimate liberty of the human conscience to be free from the dictates of the righteous.

Meanwhile, other battles for liberty were being fought. In the narrow channel the Dutch, struggling against the Spaniards, were turning the sea into freedom's ally. On the stormy Atlantic, Englishmen were fighting their battles against the Spaniards for liberty of movement and trade. And, just as Peter Wentworth symbolized one element in the struggle for liberty at home, so Sir Francis Drake symbolized it beyond the English realm. But if Drake, like Wentworth, is amongst the immortals, we should not forget that he was essentially a member of a brilliant west country contingent. These men, the great irrepressibles, a brood of cousins, half-brothers, friends, extended the reach of English overseas enterprise until, at last, Drake had encircled the great globe itself.

All this had been in prospect as long ago as Henry VIII's reign, when William Hawkins probed the African and American coasts; and, under Mary, Willoughby and Chancellor, dreaming of a north-east passage to the other side of the world, showed a way instead into the heart of Russia. But the fifteen-seventies saw, for the first time, an England staking her claim to be a front rank maritime power. Moreover, after the disaster of San Juan de Ulua in 1568, English seamen counted themselves at war with Spain, even though their queen for another two decades formally kept the peace. But she knew what they were doing, blessed their enterprises, and backed them with her funds. Better still, she sheltered them with a skilful and equivocal diplomacy, which was worth to them as much as a couple of men-of-war.

Hunting and plundering the Spaniard on land and sea, in the new world and the old became, as Dr Rowse has called it, 'a Protestant activity', crystallized in Drake's voyage of 1577. Behind him were the money and prestige of the queen's ministers, and of the queen herself. So sustained, this little fleet of five ships, with Drake in the *Pelican*, later re-named the *Golden Hind*, set out over the Atlantic, down across the equator, on again down, past the coast of Brazil. From there he pressed on round the Straits of Magellan and, at last, out into the Pacific. Long ago, Drake had prayed that, by God's grace, he might one day sail in an English ship on this great ocean. But by now the *Golden Hind* was alone.

What precisely Drake was up to remains to this day obscure. Clearly, he carried at least two sets of instructions, of which one seems to have come from the queen personally—and been kept secret from Burghley. Whether some major imperial enterprise was brewing, or whether he was directed to aim some bold strategic blow at Spanish communications, we do not know. Certainly, while his fleet was at sea there were differences of counsel on board—and the threat of mutiny. To this Drake replied with swift resolution, in the name of the queen, by the court martial and execution of Doughty, who led the opposition at sea. Then, as the *Golden Hind* sailed alone up the Pacific Coast of America, the joyous sight of a rich Spanish treasure ship came into view. The unfortunate vessel now had the memorable experience of the brave courtesy of the English commander as he firmly took possession of its wealth, with the utmost—and sincere—display of his characteristic and famous charm.

Now Drake pressed further north, 'annexed' California to the Tudor crown, sailed across the Pacific, negotiated a trade treaty with a sultan in the Moluccas and moved on into the Indian Ocean. Then with a wonderful combination of bravery, skill and luck, he sailed on for months through the southern seas, rounded the Cape of Good Hope and turned north through the Atlantic to reach Plymouth Sound in September 1580, his ship crammed with the treasure he had taken and the spices he had bought. He had circumnavigated the world and been out of touch with England for three years. His famous question on reaching home waters was: is the queen alive and well?

She was indeed; but if the distant prospect was brightened for her by his seamanship of genius, nearer home her skies were sadly overcast. Two major problems pressed for solution. To the west lay an Ireland, disrupted and seething with discontent; to the southeast the Netherlands, whose defeat by Spain would be dangerous to England, but whose victory over Spain —if achieved under French patronage—would carry dangers of its own. Of these two problems, Ireland proved the gravest and it was to baffle her as it baffled every one of her successors.

Elizabethan Ireland possessed *in excelsis* the capacity to breed—and attract—political adventurers of all sorts. It was a country economically undeveloped and culturally stagnant. It was divided up into warring clans under semi-barbaric chieftains amongst whom there occasionally emerged a momentary flicker of statesmanship, only to be snuffed out in a bloody struggle either between themselves or against the English. Most of the inhabitants (including some pockets of Scots) differed in race from their English rulers; but there was an English 'pale' along part of the coast and an upper crust of Anglo-Irish nobility, of medieval origin, whose policies—if they may be so described—helped only to make confusion worse confounded.

To such a country, Elizabeth tried, one way or another, to bring peace : sometimes by conciliation and recognition of one of the Irish leaders, such as Shane O'Neill of Ulster in 1562, and, in the same year, the Earl of Desmond of Munster. But these attempts soon collapsed as distrust, treachery and murder intervened in the negotiations. More often the English leaders used ruthless force to meet local terrorism, but did so with inadequate resources to hold the country down. In addition, in these inappropriate times, new English settlements, on the lands of excluded or evicted Irish, added further burdens to the occupying forces. By the 'seventies Elizabeth was faced with a situation of alarming dimensions.

To these personal, political and racial feuds there were now added the fierce passions of a religious revival. For the backward Irish church, poor alike in material and spirit, now received a revitalizing injection of Catholic reform. Of all Europe, it was in Ireland that the Counter-Reformation achieved one of its most spectacular successes; for it here became identified with the zeal for national independence, resisting alike the military arms and the alien church of the English garrisons, and the ramshackle administration living under their tenuous protection.

Elizabeth, who did not believe in religious wars and hated being embroiled in such conflicts, now found, in

Ireland, that she had a bitter and inveterate one on her hands. The pope's blessing—and missionaries—flowed freely to the war-torn island and, in their wake, motley crews bent on invading and liberating the country in a righteous battle, only to perish miserably in some insignificant engagement. For the moment Philip II refused to enlarge his enormous commitments with an Irish war; but the opportunity to make trouble for Elizabeth there was always inviting, and no one could tell where or when the blow would fall. By 1580 she was further from a solution that she had been in 1570.

The same applied to the Netherlands. After 1572, the Dutch rebels had begun to move back from the sea —and the security of the English ports—to the shores of their own country. Their expulsion from the southern English coast by the queen in that year may have been a genuine attempt to appease Spain as well as to protect English and friendly shipping from irresponsible Dutch attack. But, whatever its intention, its result was that the Dutch clambered in at Brill and Flushing, and from there spread out through the Low Countries, while William of Orange pushed on from Germany into Brabant, and the French threw in forces elsewhere to add to the embarrassment of Philip II. The Spanish grip on the whole territory sharply weakened, yet the Protestant victory, now in prospect, brought little pleasure to Elizabeth.

The French forces, with the battle-slogan of 'France and liberty', were intervening on the side of the Dutch

with somewhat greater fervour than the lukewarm
Elizabeth. A Dutch victory, under French patronage,
would replace the relatively weak Spanish hold on the
area by a much greater menace from neighbouring
France. French power in the channel would now reach
all the way up from Brest to Brill. Against this danger,
England was destined to fight many wars in the
centuries after the death of Elizabeth; and her attitude
therefore again forms part of the long tradition of
English diplomacy. So by a paradox her energies were
now bent on neutralizing French aid to the Dutch.
English interests—not necessarily Protestant interests—
would best be served, she believed, by a negotiated
peace between William of Orange and Philip II. But
it was not an easy policy for men like Walsingham and
Leicester to accept. She favoured Dutch liberties as did
they, but she preferred Dutch freedom safeguarded
under the weak rule of Spain rather than in a fighting
alliance between France and William of Orange. For
that reason, late in 1575 she presented herself as mediator between William and Philip II : a thankless and
abortive task.

All prospects of this were shattered in 1576 by the
'sack of Antwerp'—an outbreak of savagery by the
unpaid Spanish troops—with the result that the seventeen provinces of the Netherlands stood momentarily
as an united nation fighting Spain. All this happened
on the eve of the arrival of Don John of Austria, the
new Spanish governor of the Netherlands. Here was a

soldier of European fame, charged now with a double
mission : to re-establish peace in the Netherlands and
then to withdraw the Spanish troops *by sea,* nominally
to return to Spain, but actually to mount an attack on
the English. Peace in the Netherlands was in fact
largely restored in 1577—although William of Orange
was not a party to it—and Don John could therefore
prepare for the second phase of his design. It looked
as though the mediating, peace-loving Elizabeth had
bred a scorpion.

Fortunately for her, the scorpion's sting had to be
diverted back to the Netherlands. Mutual distrust between the governor and his subjects flared up once
again into open warfare. Once again, in spite of its
dangers, Elizabeth resumed her role of mediator. She
failed again; and the Netherlands were sucked into a
chaos of war and famine. It was at this stage that the
rebels, failing of one saviour, Elizabeth, strengthened
their trust in another, the Duke of Anjou : the man
who (as Alençon) had in 1572 begun his intermittent
labours as a suitor for Elizabeth's hand. This bankrupt, unglamorous duke seemed poorly equipped to be
either the liberator of the Netherlands or the lover of
Elizabeth. But there could be no doubt that he represented the dangerous link between these Spanish provinces and France. That link must somehow be snapped
or weakened, or the French leader diverted from his
appointed task. To achieve this Elizabeth resorted cold-
bloodedly to that outrageous, diplomatic technique

which had served her so well in the past. She reopened
the marriage negotiations with France.

At least, that is how we would interpret these
activities if we judged them simply in terms of her
past performance. But this time, whatever diplomatic
purposes the Anjou courtship was meant to serve, there
entered into it some other, disconcertingly human,
element never present during the official courtships of
the last two decades. Simier, Anjou's representative in
London, as well as a good number of Englishmen, considered that she had at last fallen in love. Many of her
subjects, in alarm, believed that the whole Netherlands
business would dwindle into insignificance as compared
with the grave crisis which such a marriage would pre-
cipitate. It was openly said that she was going to repeat
the blunders of her sister Mary by bringing an unpopular foreigner to the throne. The men who had
urged her long ago to marry and produce an heir now
seemed about to be hoist with their own petard.

In August 1579 Anjou himself visited the queen in
London. His visit was a short one but for the citizens
of the capital it was long enough and full of forboding.
A pamphleteer, John Stubbs, celebrated his departure
with a scurrilous attack on the French royal family and
a warning to the queen's subjects of the disasters that
would flow from the projected marriage. For this public
service he was sentenced to have his right hand chopped
off, after which ceremony he rose to the occasion by
lifting his hat with his left hand and uttering the loyal
prayer, 'God save the Queen'.

God alone, it must have seemed to many of her ministers, could save the queen. In the autumn of 1579, as this internal crisis came to a head Elizabeth, now aged 46, stood at the climacteric of her life and her affairs.

Chapter Seven

The Catholic Problem, 1580–4

BY the year 1580 Elizabeth's reign was half over. The excitements and the passions of her youth were almost spent, but they would flare up once or twice in a sunset tempest before she finally settled down to her high middle age. Her ministers also bore all the marks of the passing decades. Lord Burghley, now in his six-tieth year, was by the standards of the time an old man—it is hard indeed ever to think of him as really young—but he still had nearly two decades of work in him before he would lay down his white staff of the lord treasurership. The Earl of Leicester was in his early fifties; but he was not wearing so well. Good living and hard work were taking their toll, and he would not see the end of the 1580s. Sir Francis Walsingham, the queen's able and puritanical Secretary of State—as well as head of her counter-intelligence service—would out-stay him by only a short while. But the queen would outlast them all and, in the closing decade of her reign, would be confronted with unfamiliar political prob-lems in an unfamiliar national climate. The greatest test of her statesmanship was yet to come.

For, if the queen was changing, so too was the nation over which she ruled. In many ways life was improving, as contemporaries were not slow to observe. 'The furniture of our houses', wrote the Reverend William Harrison at about this time, 'also exceedeth and is grown in manner even to passing delicacy.' This increasing luxury was not simply the perquisite of one class. 'And herein I do not speak of the nobility and gentry only, but likewise of the lowest sort in most places of our south country that have anything at all to take to.' As a result, 'the wealth of our country (God be praised therefore, and give us grace to employ it well) doth infinitely appear'.

The rising standard of living was, moreover, to be seen throughout the whole range of domestic comfort. 'There are old men', he wrote, 'yet dwelling in the village where I remain, which have noted three things to be marvellously altered.' These were the increased number of chimneys, one step towards cleaner and sweeter homes; good bedding and pillows in general use; and lastly, there was the shift from wood to pewter, silver and tin in tableware. The first unmistakable habits of gentility were taking hold even of the husbandman's cottage.

Harrison, it must be confessed, tended to see things through rosy-tinted spectacles. But he was not alone in his impressions of the time. There was a buoyancy in the whole economy and society of mid-Elizabethan England: it was the confident middle age of a prospering people. The mood would pass; but, for about a decade after 1575, the trade and industry of the nation seem to have shaken off the depressions and handicaps of the early part of the reign. Famine had attended the

queen at her accession, and this had been followed by
plague which, in 1562, had struck at the queen herself. These troubles, and difficulties in the overseas
trade with Flanders, had darkened the opening years of
her rule. Then, after some alleviation, had come trade
war, political troubles at home, bad harvests. There
had been brief intervals when depression had lifted;
but it was not until about 1575 that the tide of prosperity really turned, and it flowed for another decade
in England's favour. Of course, poverty, hunger and
unemployment were never wholly out of sight or mind.
But economic activity was at a higher level than for
some years past; and, for a time, the queen governed a
smiling land.

That same buoyancy was manifested in literature as
well. Spenser and Sidney, at about this period, were
making their glorious experiments in verse from which
their young contemporary, Shakespeare, would one day
advance to the unconquerable peaks of English literature. In 1577 had come Holinshed's *Chronicles*, in
1579 North's translation of Plutarch's *Lives* (both
works destined to be re-enacted in some of the greatest
of Shakespeare's plays); and, a decade later, Christo-
pher Marlowe would sing his praise of the eager years
of English thought and culture, of

> *Our souls, whose faculties can comprehend*
> *The wondrous architecture of the world,*
> *And measure every wandering planet's course,*
> *Still climbing after knowledge infinite ...*

This great literary movement drew many of its roots from the vigorous citizens of the capital who, from 1576 onwards, had their own theatre, from which would soon be trumpeted—in historic and romantic drama—the ebullient patriotism of a proud nation. It is perhaps as well to remember, in view of what would happen to the theatre in the next century, that in its formative years it took its sustenance and encouragement from the ordinary Londoner at his recreation. Aristocratic patrons, of course, there were. The Earl of Leicester had his 'men'; so did his brother, the Earl of Warwick, and there were a number of others. But the playwrights—not only Shakespeare but, for example, Greene and Peele and Marlowe—knew their London well, not least its sordid fringe, and they gave the groundlings their full pennyworth of poetry and excitement. Like the music hall of the late nineteenth century, the Elizabethan public theatre found its inspiration in the rough gaiety of English urban life.

But this vigour and buoyancy was not confined to the world of drama. It showed itself in the bold affirmations of aggressive puritanism. It was heard in the debates of the Tudor parliaments. It drove Elizabethan seamen with a restless and resourceful impetus into the seven seas. It gave inspiration and courage to the Catholic revival of the period.

The papal bull of deposition, promulgated in 1570, had proved itself a profitless political weapon, a boomerang rather than an executioner's sword. It had armed the Elizabethan government against its Catholic subjects who now stood committed (under direction of the bull) to treason against the queen. A papal gloss upon it, issued ten years later, was designed to extract them from this predicament. It said that Catholics were in fact instructed not to rise in rebellion until the time was ripe. This made matters worse. It was as though it affirmed again that the queen held the throne only on suffrance during the pope's pleasure. In fact the solution was not found in the close logic of the Curia but in the characteristic pragmatism of the English. Apart from a few extremists, most Catholics did their best to serve God and the queen.

But they longed none the less for the spiritual comforts of their faith, the Mass and the sacraments, the confession, the absolution. The surviving Catholic priests, the remnants from the great days of Mary, were dying out. For many Catholics the services of a priest were no longer to be had. Already under pressure of penal legislation, there were clear signs of a drift into the established Church. The ultimate extinction of the old Church, leaderless and without organization, was within sight. At this stage Catholicism in England was saved by its young men.

For a decade, some of the best among them had been drawn to the training colleges for priests established on friendly soil abroad : to Douai, the first of these, founded in 1568—whence the college moved to Rheims in 1578—to the English college at Rome founded in that year, to Valladolid in 1589 and elsewhere. These were the famous seminaries; and the term 'seminary priest' to English Protestant ears brought the dread prospect of Romish intolerance. Not all the missionary priests were Jesuits. The early ones were not; but from 1580 the Jesuit order held a prominent position in the movement. These men, hardened like steel in the seven years' discipline of their college, were not sacrificing their lives for Rome but for England; they were giving all so that their Protestant countrymen might be spared the long torments of damnation to which their wilful heresy must surely lead.

As priests, after 1585, they would be officially branded as traitors. When caught they often paid, even before then, the full penalty of treason. But many, many times, before they even set foot in England, they went over in their mind's eye each revolting ritual of the traitor's death: to be dragged through the streets tied to the back of a cart; to be hanged; to be cut down while still alive; to endure the death agonies of unspeakable mutilation while half-conscious; and finally to be quartered. The executioner, even in these last minutes of butchery, held no surprises for the condemned priest. Now, as so many times before in anticipation, he re-enacted in his Elizabethan Calvary the last hours of Christ. It was his appointed destiny; and, amidst the squalor of the bestial scene, his martyr's crown shone all the brighter.

The historian, like so many of the martyr's contemporaries, even as he admires the heroic self-sacrifice, falters in trying to analyse the outlook of these priests. He feels that it needs other disciplines, perhaps those of the psychologist and the anthropologist, to explain the passion for martyrdom, the death-wish, the fears of some that they might not be granted the beatific joys of a martyr's death. For example, one woman, a chronic invalid, repeatedly told her priest: 'I naturally want more than anything to die for Christ, but it is too much to hope that it will be by the executioner's hand.' She gained from one of her confessors the promise that 'if God should make him worthy of that glorious end, he would pray for her that she might obtain the like happiness'. In due course she gained her wish. 'She received the sentence of death with manifest joy and thankfulness,' and kissed the gallows on which she was executed.

For people like this the policy of brutality was a failure. More men sought admission to the colleges than the accommodation could hold. Many of them came from families of the highest repute. Few of them were found hesitant when the long-awaited hour came. From among so many we need to choose only three examples.

The first is Edmund Campion, the gentle scholar, eloquent, patient, dignified, who aroused the love of his adherents and the respect of his enemies. He was executed in 1581. The second is Robert Southwell, the young poet of the highest promise. In 1595 he expiated his grandfather's seizure of Catholic monastic land in laying down his own life in the hope that Catholicism in this country might once again be restored to its place. Long before his death he had translated—and transmuted—a poem by Tasso which was to be his own memorial :

> *Then crop the morning rose while it is fair;*
> *Our day is short, the evening makes it die.*
> *Yield God the prime of youth ere it impair,*
> *Lest He the dregs of crooked age deny.*

Father John Gerard, our third example, was cast from a different mould. He, too, like Campion and Southwell, was a Jesuit. But there was nothing of the dreamer in him. His genius lay elsewhere: as an organizer and propagandist of immense skill. He detected at once that, if he could revive the flickering Catholic spirit in the country houses of the upper middle class, from there it would be carried to neighbours, dependants, friends until the English counties would at last be ready for the open restoration of the old faith. Here is his own account of one such conquest.

He visited a landed family in the north of England just as it was about to go on a hunt. His host begged him to join it because one of its members, not a Catholic himself, had recently married into the family. This was a wonderful opportunity to win him over. After some hesitation Gerard agreed; and, 'all day I rode alongside him—the huntsman whom I was hunting down myself. Whenever the pack was at fault and stopped giving tongue, I used the pause to follow up my own little chase, and gave tongue myself in real earnest.' So it went on, with Gerard skilfully turning each aspect of the hunt into a parable about sin and salvation. 'But it was only after much talking that I made any impression on his will. All that day and the next I worked on him. On the fourth day he gave in and became a Catholic.' This at last was total victory; and it brought prospects of other converts as well. 'He is practising his religion still and often keeps priests in his house and introduces them to other families.'

Who were more dangerous to the government of Elizabeth : pure idealists like Campion and Southwell, or subtle ideologues like Gerard or Robert Parsons, who had nothing to learn from—and a good deal to teach —the skilled propagandists of a later age? Southwell converted by example, Gerard by creating Catholic cells up and down the country, even in prison in which, in due course, he was able to establish a chapel, hear confessions, and administer the sacraments. Both men were dangerous to the established order; and the government, in a blind fear of unseen enemies, struck at them with clumsy and brutal hands.

Did the missionaries succeed? From all over England, in the late 1570s, came evidence of growing resistance. 'A more stiff-necked, wilful or obstinate people did I never know or hear of,' said Sandys, Archbishop of York, of the Catholic recusants of his city. 'Rebellion is rampant, attendance at church is contemptuous,' said his colleague of Hereford. 'My Lord of Canterbury and I', wrote the Bishop of London to Sir Francis Walsingham, 'have received from divers of our brethren, bishops of this realm, [information] that the papists do marvellously increase, both in number and in obstinately withdrawing of themselves from the church and service of God.' To put them in prison, he added, had availed little except to save them housekeeping money. Sterner legislation was necessary, the bishop believed, and the queen must be made *animo obfirmato* —of resolute mind—or 'our labour will be lost'.

As long as Catholicism was dependent wholly upon native resources, it might have been contained and worn down. A generation would arise which had no memory of Catholic England. But now a new leadership was coming back from abroad; powerful, confident, an army of men among whom ten rose for each one that fell. In 1581 the government accepted the view that it could not fight the new battles with the old weapons it had created a generation ago.

In that year Parliament had before it a bill against recusancy, far more savage than the legislation of 1559. It struck at both the missionaries and their converts. It struck also at the wealthy Catholic households where the missionaries found their safest harbour. Anyone converting the queen's subjects to Catholicism, or allowing himself so to be converted, was guilty of treason for which, of course, the penalty was death. Here again was the policy of containment, but backed this time with Draconian measures. Anyone simply refusing to attend church was to pay £20 each month for his abstinence.

These were harsh proposals; but they derived from harsh circumstances. With the coming of the Catholic missionaries, the Counter-Reformation at last breached the English coast, with its forces fanning out across the shires. And Mary, Queen of Scots, although a prisoner, was believed ready to complete the good work begun by the missionaries. The English air, for the next few years, was thick with plots and rumours of plots. Abroad, the 'Enterprise of England' was in preparation, with Philip II and the pope as its lay and spiritual patrons. In 1579 a body of troops had, in the name of the papacy, landed in Ireland (but for them, as for their English enemies, Ireland proved unconquerable.) In 1582 a Jesuit inspired conference was held in France to work out in detail an invasion of England from a Catholic-controlled Scotland. In such circumstances, and in spite of the undoubtedly sincere affirmations of most of the missionaries that their aims were exclusively religious, Parliament could only regard their work as an aspect of political warfare, the softening up of the nation before the military offensive was launched.

Yet, even in this time of peril the queen succeeded in urging calmer counsel on her ministers and parliamentarians. Their hostile bill against the missionaries survived; but it was significantly changed. To convert or be converted to Catholicism was, as the act finally emerged, not treasonable unless it could be shown that it would be followed by treasonable acts. The onus was on the prosecution to prove that conversion was—as the act put it—*for that intent*, namely to withdraw her subjects from lawful obedience to the queen. Once again she tried to take the issue out of religion and put it back into politics, where it belonged.

Yet, even so modified, the act had a mortal sharpness. It sought to cut away the Catholic leadership, spiritual and secular, from the followers. It struck at their faith and their estates, for the £20 fine remained; and if they did not pay their fines within three months they could be committed to prison. In 1587 the act was strengthened to enable the government, in case of default, to seize—and retain until the debt was paid— two-thirds of a recusant's lands and all his property. Yet the act remained faulty in its operation. For example, only one person in Essex—where there were a good number of influential Catholics—paid the full fine. And, in some instances, the queen personally intervened to lighten the burden. But others paid heavily with their wealth and their happiness.

Still the queen strove, wherever possible, to isolate religion from politics. Her most eminent minister, Lord Burghley, also claimed to be doing precisely that, as he declared in a tract of the time :

> And though there are many subjects known in the realm that differ in some opinions of religion from the Church of England, and that do also not forbear to profess the same, yet in that they do also profess loyalty and obedience to Her Majesty and offer readily in Her Majesty's defence to impugn and resist any foreign force, though it should come or be procured from the pope himself, none of these sort are, for their contrary opinions in religion, prosecuted or charged with any crimes or pains of treason, nor yet willingly searched in their consciences for their contrary opinions that savour not of treason.

We should not overrate such affirmations. Burghley had no love for the Catholic religion; and the most that he hoped for was that the passage of time rather than the hangman's noose would end a movement whose leaders were proscribed and whose morale was broken. Here, as in so much else, queen and minister spoke the same language; and, in the mood of the day, they stand out as moderates. But royal theory was far ahead of local practice. In some districts a self-righteous para-noiac like Richard Topcliffe could leave a trail of dread and misery in the Catholic homes of the queen's subjects.

Fortunately the average Protestant Englishman had not much use for men like Richard Topcliffe. And when, at last, he overreached himself, the government itself laid Topcliffe by the heels. But this is not to say that the average Catholic lived in peace. Some of the smaller fry continued to be fined twelvepence for each week of recusancy; some for failure to pay were still cast into prison. But, in general, it was the wealthy and prominent Catholics who were attacked with heavy fines, with imprisonment, with severe restraints in their public and professional lives. In a number of cases they suffered serious damage in their family fortunes and prospects.

Yet, when all has been said in criticism of these acts, they must still be set in the climate of the time. While the Catholic missionaries, and their harbourers, were paying their penalties for organized dissent, English Protestant sailors were sweating their lives away as

Spanish galley slaves, or dying at the stake in some torrid Spanish American city. To English eyes Philip II's imperialism and the Inquisition came together, dressed in the gentle clothes of the missionary priests. The bloody memories of half a century of Spanish intolerance obscured for most Englishmen the nobility of Catholic idealism. In order to get the whole matter into perspective, it should perhaps be added that, throughout the sixteenth century, it was safer to be a Spanish Catholic in London than an English Protestant in Madrid.

We should remember also that these religious issues were prominent at the very time when Elizabeth's whole diplomatic edifice threatened to collapse into fragments, and the Spanish power was still further enlarged. In 1580 the King of Portugal died, and Philip II laid claim to, and seized, his throne and empire. In 1581, when Elizabeth made a move to help Don Antonio, the Portuguese Pretender, Philip II threatened war.

In Scotland the situation was changing too. The son of Mary, Queen of Scots, the boy king, James VI, had for long reigned under Protestant tutelage and English patronage. But now a palace revolution brought Esme Stuart, Earl of Lennox, a Catholic Francophile, to power in Edinburgh. No one seriously believed that Scotland could rise out of its squalid factional warfare to pursue an independent policy; but the threatened re-emergence of French influence in the northern king-

dom menaced the security system so patiently erected
by Elizabeth and her ministers.

Nor were developments in the Netherlands any more
to her taste. The Dutch leader, William of Orange, had
been declared a traitor by Philip II in 1580. The Duke
of Alençon, in between his periods of courtship of Queen
Elizabeth, was leading French intervention forces in
the Netherlands, ostensibly in the interests of the Dutch
people. Elizabeth liked the French in the Netherlands
about as much as she liked the thought of them in Scotland. She preferred, at least for the time being, that
Alençon's interests should once again be anchored to
London. In April 1581, therefore, a new French marriage delegation was received in London. But it carried
away little for its pains.

By now, indeed, the Alençon marriage had passed
out of its emotional context. There was no longer any
sign of the fierce inward conflict which had tormented
the queen—and therefore her ministers—in the preceding year. Perhaps John Stubbs had not written—
and suffered for—his pamphlet in vain. Perhaps war
seemed much nearer now than ever before, too near
for the personal adventures of a courtship. Perhaps the
natural passage of time had channelled the queen's
emotions into calmer waters. In early or middle forties
it is still possible for a man or woman to cling to the
hem of youth, to hope that those things which did not
come sooner may yet come. But in the late forties one
is truly middle aged. The sun is still high in the sky;
but at last comes acknowledgement that the exacting

pressures of the early decades have lost something of their force; that some ambitions—public or private—will never be fulfilled; that some things which have not come may never come. But if these are at last yielded up, in their place may come, for the first time, the late blossoms of tranquillity.

So it was with the queen. As a result, the Alençon marriage project assumed the pattern of all its predecessors, the now classical shape of a diplomatic courtship. The queen said that she could not marry him at this stage because it would commit England openly to the Netherlands war in which he was involved. (At the same time she was careful not to break off the negotiation and thereby let in a Spanish princess, the alternative bride for the duke.) In November 1581 Alençon came once more to England and stayed three months. But now the queen he found waiting for him in London was not a lover—but an actress; and he was wasting his time. But not wholly. When he returned to the Netherlands he had obtained the queen's money, though not the queen's hand. With that he passes out of our story, to confusion and defeat in the Netherlands, to sickness and finally death, in the summer of 1584.

He had had his day; and his use had been fulfilled. Now the times were changing. England was inexorably moving from diplomacy to war. Neither Elizabeth nor Philip had wanted it : she recognizing it for the expensive gamble it was; he bogged down in the Netherlands and loaded with an intolerable burden of imperial commitments. But the logic of events, and the pressure of a warlike generation, were taking the initiative from the two rulers. 'Would to God!' Elizabeth had once said, 'that each had his own and was at peace.' Both she and Philip continued to hope for appeasement; both moved into battle with reluctant feet.

But first came the diplomatic rupture. The wild Jesuit plan of 1582 to take the British Isles *via* Scotland rested upon a false and exuberant interpretation of the rapidly changing political scene in that country. The overthrow of the Catholic ruling clique there blasted the flimsy hopes of the Jesuit plotters; and, leaving the Catholic and Protestant factions in Scotland to their game of political see-saw, they turned to what looked like the more fertile soil of the southern kingdom.

The exact extent of Catholic hostility in England to Elizabeth it is impossible to estimate. Certainly, over a large part of northern England the old faith was still strong with a considerable section of the people, including the justices of the peace and the nobility. But this is by no means the same as saying that they were ripe for rebellion. Only the Armada—if successful—would test that feeling. In the event, during the tense weeks of waiting for its coming, there was no echo among Catholic Englishmen at home of the hostile policies of the émigrés. But until the Armada year the exact extent of Catholic loyalty was anybody's guess. And, among those who guessed wrongly were the plotter Francis Throckmorton and his ally Mendoza, the Spanish ambassador in London.

Throckmorton's plot was an elaborate affair, reaching in one direction to Mary, Queen of Scots and, in the other, through the Spanish and French embassies, to the Duke of Guise in France but, *en route*, unwittingly including Sir Francis Walsingham and the English counter-espionage service. On the eve of its unfolding, it was preceded by an irrelevant curtain-raiser. In October 1583 John Somerville left Warwickshire for London, announcing to the world that he was on his way to kill the queen. He did not get anywhere near her; as an example of disinterested private enterprise his effort proved a lamentable failure.

But Throckmorton's plot, finally exposed in the same month, was the most dangerous threat that had faced the queen since the rising of the northern earls in 1569. The captured documents contained plenty of names of men expected to lead the rebellion, and of harbours where the invading fleet should land. Under torture Throckmorton confessed; and, in January 1584, the Spanish ambassador was given his passport. He was the last Spanish diplomat to be accredited to the court of Queen Elizabeth. Both his master and the queen had been overtaken by events.

Chapter Eight

The Overtures of War, 1584–7

SLOWLY, unwillingly, Elizabeth acknowledged the logic of the situation. To her, indeed, war was *ultima ratio*—the final stage in the process of reasoning, in fact the abandonment of reasoning altogether for other methods of international relations. She was a better diplomat than warrior; and perhaps she knew it. For years she had resisted this last step, a step which some of her ministers, like Leicester and Walsingham, considered inevitable. She was not yet at war but, with the diplomatic rupture of 1584, peace hung by a thread. That thread was snapped, neither by Elizabeth nor Philip, but by a tragic event in the Netherlands. For, on July 10, 1584, William the Silent, the statesman-soldier, the Protestant leader of Dutch resistance, was shot by a fanatic.

'Better late than never' had been Philip II's comment, when the news was brought to him. To Elizabeth and her parliamentarians it was an event more shattering even than the slaughter of St Bartholomew's Day, a dozen years before. It meant that, if a leaderless Netherlands finally broke before superior Spanish forces, the whole Elizabethan security system would collapse. Philip II would have in the Netherlands a dagger pointing at the heart of England. The assassina-

tion had also a more intimate lesson to teach : namely,
that men—and rulers—were mortal. Elizabeth's life
had been in danger over and over again. She had
always escaped, it is true; but so had William the
Silent—on all occasions but the last. Who dared say
that good fortune, which deserted William, would ac-
company Elizabeth all the way to the end. If it did not,
then two other members of the dramatic cast were
waiting in the wings to take part in the performance :
Mary, Queen of Scots—and civil war.

Desperate times bred desperate remedies; and it is
hardly possible, therefore, to judge the next development by the accepted standards of political morality.
To Englishmen the assassination of William underlined
the warning of Throckmorton's plot. As a consequence,
throughout the summer and autumn of 1584, Elizabeth's ministers brooded over the danger to the queen
and therefore to the nation as a whole; and they passed
back and forth schemes for political security. In essence,
they were seeking for two things : primarily, to shelter
the queen from the assassin and secondly, to serve
notice on Mary, Queen of Scots and her supporters
that, if she became involved in another plot—successful
or unsuccessful—it would be her last. She would never
rule as queen of England. They would pursue her to
the death. Common law would give place to mob vengeance.

To shelter the queen in her person there was little
that they could do beyond their usual precautions :
maintain a powerful household guard and, in the wider

sphere, an elaborate counter-espionage system to root out the plotters before their plans were ripe. But now they added a new safeguard. They would meet threat by threat. Elizabethan leaders drew up a bond—more appropriate to the Scottish than the English scene—in which they swore that if Mary instigated a plot against Elizabeth's life, *or even if such a plot were instigated without Mary's knowledge*, they would destroy Mary by any means they found to hand. They would also bar all her heirs and descendants—there was only one, James VI—from the throne of England. In so deciding, it must be stressed, they were opening the gate, in the event of Elizabeth's murder, to the possibility of civil war; for no one knew the latent strength at home and abroad behind Mary's claim. It is a chilling thought to call to mind that these eminent statesmen would prefer to plunge England into a period of bloody warfare rather than see a second Catholic Mary sit on the throne of England.

Civil war, of course, they hoped to avoid by this clear warning to Mary and her friends that they would lose more than they gained by the next attempt on Elizabeth's life. Just the same, in declaring that Elizabeth's assassination would be followed by Mary's and if necessary terrible internal strife, they had to show that they meant precisely what they said; that they were not engaged in wild and empty threats. So they decided to make their bond much more than a ministerial resolution of policy. They determined to enlarge it into a testament of the whole nation, committing itself to destroy Mary if its own queen were threatened or destroyed. Here was a chance to demonstrate to all Europe where precisely England now stood.

That autumn the bond was sent throughout the country, to come back soon after with thousands of seals and signatures of affirmation. If this was not enough as a manifesto of national opinion, the new Parliament, which assembled late in November 1584, sought to erect it into a statute. But the Bond of Association, in its original form, could have no place in the constitutional framework of England. It was essentially a declaration of what men pledged themselves to do: it was simply a policy for action at a moment of danger. How could a statute authorize the murder of a claimant to the throne—who might be innocent—and that without judicial proceedings or any established system to discover where guilt lay and what punishment was appropriate?

At this stage moderate opinion in Parliament tried to soften the mood of vengeance out of which the bond had been conceived. The inspirer of a new plot, it was argued, should be put on trial rather than submitted to an unconstitutional act of violence. Her heir should not automatically be placed under the ban of succession. This new approach encountered a good deal of resistance; but those who favoured moderation found in Elizabeth herself their most powerful ally. To her it must have been clear enough that not only was it unjust to condemn James out of hand; it was also impolitic. It would destroy the Anglo-Scottish *entente* and send

James careering after allies amongst the enemies of
Elizabeth. It would also—if effective—postpone the
ultimate unification of the two kingdoms.

The Act which finally emerged claimed the best of
both worlds. It set up an august tribunal to try any
claimant to the throne who engaged in any design
against the royal person, or was privy to one. Punishment was not to take place without a trial. So much
the moderates gained. But the statute also declared
that, once such guilt had been established, then all the
queen's subjects 'shall and may lawfully by virtue of
this act, *by all forcible and possible means*[1] pursue to
death every such wicked person'. In its concluding sentence the statute took the Bond of Association within
its framework, declaring that it 'shall and ought to be
in all things expounded and adjudged according to
the true intent and meaning of this act'. Certainly the
parliamentarians took away the incentive to mob action without trial which the bond had given. Otherwise the government itself would have faced great
instability: the first rumour of a plot would have
brought out all sorts of irregular forces bent on vengeance. But the bond in one sense was strengthened.
It was now fortified by statute; and it confirmed that
those who had taken it were morally obliged to carry
out their commitments—namely to put Mary to death
(once she was found guilty) without further warrant
from the government. This obligation Elizabeth's
ministers may have deliberately put into the statute,

[1] Author's italics.

perhaps at the queen's direction. Certainly, she would remember it in her time of stress, and remind them of their oaths.

At the same time Parliament struck again at the Catholic priests. All who had been ordained since the accession of Elizabeth—that is, ordained abroad—were to leave the country within forty days. A seminary priest who stayed here beyond that time, or who came henceforth into the realm, was to be guilty of high treason. From now onwards, to be a priest (other than one of the scattered survivors of the Marian period) was *ipso facto* to bring into action the full force of the treason laws. With such a measure, though it was that of a beleaguered nation blocking every gap in its defences, Parliament struck hardest at the Catholic religion. Hitherto it could be argued, even after the severities of the 1581 act, that men's religious consciences were free, even if they ran serious risks, and had to pay heavily, for hearing the Mass or refusing to attend the parish church. But the 1585 act went further. It aimed at the ultimate elimination of the priesthood and therefore the end of the Mass, and all Catholic ceremonial, in England. Against all her instincts and policy, the queen found herself driven, not to deny freedom of conscience—that was still intact—but to make impossible the practical expression of men's consciences in the traditional forms of their religion. If the act could be enforced—and it was a big 'if' over large tracts of northern England where the

queen's religious writ did not run—it was the gravest
blow ever aimed at Catholicism in England.

Such a policy, of course, cannot be defended in the
context of modern European ideas about toleration.
But, to the overwhelming majority of Elizabethans, it
needed no other justification than the security of their
queen. 'The good felicity and comfort of the whole
estate of this realm', they said in the Bond of Association statute of this year, 'consisteth (only next under
God) in the surety and preservation of the Queen's
most excellent Majesty.' To them that was all that
mattered.

But legislation at home was clearly not enough. The
Netherlands dagger must be turned back on the
Spaniard who wielded it. If there are any general rules
of war, then the most fundamental of all is surely that
the battles should be fought, if possible, on foreign soil.
The best line of defence may ultimately be found at
home—for us the frontier waters of the channel—but
home defence is the last defence. And it may not always
be the strongest. In any case, it would have been a
dereliction of statesmanship to have waited for Philip's
armies to devour piecemeal the broken fragments of
the Netherlands resistance and let him prepare for the
greater feast across the channel. For England, open
intervention on the side of the Dutch became, after the
death of William the Silent, indispensable. But it carried enormous hazards in its train.

To many Englishmen the hazards were worth
accepting, for the bitter struggle in the Netherlands

was now intimately bound up with their own liberties. Their idealism as well as their interests seemed to demand that Elizabeth should throw in her reserves of men and treasure into what had become, in fact though not in name, the common cause against Spain. Most of Elizabeth's Privy Council shared that view: she must now strike hard against Spain in the Netherlands before the build-up against England was complete. Under Alexander of Parma, one of the great generals of the age, the Spaniards were pushing the Dutch from one line of defence after another. Brussels was falling: other strategic cities were going the same way. Across the border, in France, the Catholic League was now openly allied with Spain, and the battle for the French throne was fully joined. There was no nation but England to which the beleaguered Dutch could turn for help.

Still Elizabeth tarried. Still she looked for negotiations with Spain. Still the ephemeral prospects of appeasement beckoned her on. Yet, at the very time when the pacific spirit within her was trying to reassert its mastery, Philip II at last resolved to throw his full weight into the Enterprise of England, as it was called, namely the destruction of its religious liberty and political independence.

For him the diplomatic position had vastly improved. The coming extinction of Netherlands resistance, and his rising influence in France, persuaded him that the propitious moment for the attack on England was at hand. This, and the imminent failure of the Spanish corn supplies in 1585, induced him to lay hands on the English merchant ships in Spanish ports, engaged upon their lawful tasks of carrying corn there, under the illusory guarantee of safe-conduct given by the Spanish government itself. That was in May 1585. In June, in response, the Netherlands envoys were received by Elizabeth. The brutal treachery of this Spanish stroke was at last galvanizing her into action. In August, but not without a good deal of heartsearching, she concluded a treaty with the Netherlands, promising an army of assistance. In September, Sir Francis Drake sailed from Plymouth, nominally to obtain the release of the English ships in Spanish ports, but (with the tacit approval of the queen) to strike also at Spain and her possessions wherever opportunity offered.

This was war; and, if we are looking for a turning-point in Elizabeth's reign, this is surely it. She was now 52 years of age and, although she had 18 years left to live and reign, she would never know peace again. Her hopes of maintaining stability and security by diplomatic means had turned to ashes. Her policy of strict economy and narrow commitments died with them. Her resolution to live within her income and, wherever possible, to do without parliamentary taxation—and therefore unsolicited parliamentary advice—was no longer tenable. Now she must stretch and strain her resources almost to breaking-point, live on her capital, scrape around for all manner of revenue, inefficient and unpopular, which would one day whip up her parliamentarians to a white anger. Now she must watch the very men who bade her take aggressive measures dissipate her limited means in fruitless engagements.

A liberating army always occupies an ambiguous position on the territory of the power it proposes to liberate. It has come, as both parties know, not simply out of a brotherly love for its comrades in arms, but because the nation which sends it believes that its own liberty will be secured in the combined effort. Therefore, it is expected to pay its way and, it is hoped, pay something towards the cost of the home army which has hitherto fought alone in the common cause. Also, as time passes, the liberating army, subtly and unintentionally, takes on the shape of an occupying army to the people in whose territory it lives. In the end, the very people who have called for the liberating force long to be delivered from their liberators.

When the Dutch envoys came to Elizabeth in the summer of 1585, they eagerly offered her the full sovereignty of the Netherlands. That expensive honour she courteously declined. But she undertook to send some 6,000 men and a further 1,000 to hold the 'cautionary' towns, handed over by the Dutch as assurances that their debts to her would be repaid. In December 1585 Leicester set sail for the Netherlands; and, although he knew that the queen was resolved not to be caught up in the complex internal politics of that country, he promptly accepted the office of Governor-General. An angry queen sent him the harsh messages he deserved; but she also sent him money and supplies —apparently never enough. So the heroism of war was submerged in the two-way traffic of recrimination, Elizabeth telling her commander that she was getting scanty returns for large expenditure, her commander lamenting that he could never implement his obligations while he was kept perilously short of supplies.

'My cause', wrote Leicester to Walsingham, 'was not nor is other than the Lord and the queen. If the queen fail, yet must I trust in the Lord; and on him I see I am wholly to depend.' Not wholly. Out of the queen's money, the Governor-General raised his *own* pay by nearly 80 per cent. Two years of half-hearted warfare in the Netherlands cost the queen over £300,000, much of it drained away in mismanagement and corruption. 'It is a sieve', she cried, 'that spends, as it receives, to little purpose.' But the war had its glories too, including the memorable incident of Sir Philip Sidney's heroic death at Zutphen. The dispatch reporting his death to Philip II in Spain has on it a marginal note in the king's own hand. 'He was my godson,' he wrote : surely one of the best and briefest comments on the tragic costs of war.

Compared with the failures in the Netherlands, Drake's privateering attacks upon Spain and her communications promised better rewards. True, there were no large bounties to be shared out this time, but Drake revealed again that on their natural element, the sea, the English could always give a good account of themselves. None the less, the queen's governing resolution was not to scatter her resources in face of the coming attack from Spain upon England itself. Nor could the failures of Leicester—or even the successes of Drake—dissuade her from her settled conviction that her best safeguards lay in diplomacy. And to diplomacy she now returned.

Above all she must be secure on her only land frontier, that with Scotland in the north. In 1586 the ever turbulent Scottish political scene settled down to relative stability; and in the summer of that year James VI signed a treaty of alliance with Elizabeth, each promising the other full aid in the event of invasion by a foreign power. In addition, James received from the queen an allowance of £4,000 a year. To Elizabeth it must have seemed money far better spent than the sum, nearly forty times as much, seeping away in the watery plains of the Netherlands.

In signing the treaty of Berwick in July 1586, James VI may have unintentionally signed the death-warrant of his mother, Mary, Queen of Scots. For, by that treaty, he came nearer than ever before to recognition as the acknowledged successor of Elizabeth, although, as always, no official word was spoken to that effect. The treaty brought him an income; it brought probably with it the realization that his closest friend was his nearest neighbour. But it inevitably, by its very nature, went further to isolate Mary than any step previously taken by her son. For the time was shortly coming when the unhappy James would have to weigh in the balance the treaty, the pension of £4,000,

security and the succession against the life of an adult-
erous mother from whom he had been separated almost
at birth.

If, in this respect, James's position was unenviable,
Elizabeth's was no better. For since 1585 she had been
poised very delicately on the edge of one of the great
crises of her reign. The main policy of her ministers,
underwritten by Parliament in that year, had been laid
down. If Mary were again involved in a plot against
Elizabeth, Mary would be destroyed. Every constitutional gap through which she might escape had been
blocked. It was as though Mary were surrounded by a
minefield : one false step on her part would blow her
headlong to her appointed fate. If there is much in her
character to provoke criticism, there is also in it a good
deal of pathos, not least in the second half of 1586,
as we see her walking blindly to her own destruction.
During these months English privy councillors watched
her progress with cautious pleasure; but for Elizabeth
herself there could be no joy in the proceedings.

It was Sir Francis Walsingham who guarded the
trap, but Mary herself who assured it of success. In the
summer of 1586 Anthony Babington, the latest of a
line of young and gallant conspirators who thought
enthusiasm an adequate substitute for intelligence, began his plot to murder Elizabeth, release Mary with
the help of a foreign army, and place her on the
English throne. These proposals were soon familiar to
Walsingham since, unknown to Mary, all her correspondence was passing through official channels before

being transmitted to her castle-prison. Babington was so foolish as to ask her to give her personal approval to the plot; and Mary, even more foolish, put her delighted assent into writing, including with it a discussion of the strategy of an invading army. That was all that Walsingham needed, except the names of a few more of the conspirators. He politely asked Babington for this information by having a forged postcript added to Mary's letter; but Walsingham could not wait for an answer. He acted in August. Babington and his friends were arrested and, under examination, revealed the complicity of Mary. She was tried under the already established procedure and found guilty. The whole thing had worked with almost clockwork precision.

Because of this, it has sometimes been alleged that the plot was bogus and Mary's letter to Babington a forgery arranged by Walsingham. But the leading modern scholars, Protestant and Catholic alike, do not hold that opinion, however much they may differ about the methods used by Walsingham, or the justice of the sentence now to be passed on Mary. And it was not only Mary who was caught in a trap. In the ensuing months Elizabeth herself would be the prisoner of a situation not of her own making.

Had she wished, Elizabeth could have allowed the proceedings from now on to follow the due process of the 1584 statute, with herself formally signing the inevitable warrant of execution. From such a step she shrank in horror, while her ministers watched with dismay as she hesitated on the brink of decision. If she refused to sign the warrant, all their patient labours could be neutralized at the last. 'I fear more slackness in Her Majesty', wrote Burghley, 'than will stand either with her surety [security] or with ours. God direct her heart to follow faithful counsel.'

Elizabeth's tortured hesitations were intensified by the letters she was receiving from Scotland. At first James had scarcely thought that his mother was in peril of her life. He assumed, of course, that her conditions of imprisonment would grow stricter; and he observed coldly that she must now drink the ale she had brewed. He added the helpful suggestion that the best thing that she could do now was to devote herself to spiritual affairs. But once it became clear that Mary's latest plot would also be her last, he sought by every means, in letter and embassy, to convey to Elizabeth his own intense—and I think, genuine—horror at the prospect. In this he was supported by the opinion of the Scottish people, speaking now in a rare moment of unity.

As a son he pleaded for his mother; as an ally he begged Elizabeth not to destroy a treaty of such value to them both. But as a king he seemed to touch her most nearly. 'What law of God', he asked, 'can permit that justice shall strike upon them whom He has appointed supreme dispensators of the same [law] under Him?' Monarchs, he reminded Elizabeth, had been called gods by God himself. Their 'anointing by God cannot be defiled by man, unrevenged by the Author thereof'. Monarchs 'being supreme and immediate lieutenant[s] of God in Heaven, cannot therefore be judged by their equals in earth. What monstrous thing is it', he warned her, 'that sovereign princes themselves should be the example givers of their own sacred diadems profaning!'

That was the crux of the matter. Whatever common humanity moved Elizabeth at this juncture, it was strongly reinforced by her own conception of kingship as something out of reach of the ordinary legal processes which applied to the rest of mankind. To consent to the execution of one who had sat on the thrones of Scotland and France was to devalue kingship itself, to betray the Tudor heritage, to attaint God's anointed. She was in effect being asked by her ministers to grant royal confirmation that monarchs could be punished as other men; to sanction a concept—although no one at the time could have realized it—under which an English king would be judicially executed in 1649 and a French one in 1793. The royal appeal from James to his sister monarch found a disquieting echo in Elizabeth's responding mind.

But we must break into her musings to observe that James, at this time, was engaging in a species of political double-talk. While these powerful messages were being sent, he was also maintaining private contacts; and through one of these Leicester learned—as did, no doubt, other ministers—that James was not prepared to destroy the treaty to save his mother. Moreover, in a personal letter to Leicester, James, after wholly dis-

sociating himself from Mary's activities, added this
curious remark : 'how fond [foolish] and inconstant I
were if I should prefer my mother to the title let all
men judge'. The word 'prefer' must have been carefully chosen, for the sentence admitted of two mean-
ings. It could be taken simply as a declaration that he
would not 'prefer' his mother to the throne of England
before his own succession, that he did not acknowledge
that her title carried precedence over his own. But it
could also mean that he would not 'prefer' her in such
a way as to break the alliance; in short, that he would
not allow his desire to save his mother's life to cancel
the treaty and therefore exclude him from the succession. In this second sense Leicester and Elizabeth read
the message. Subsequent events showed that their interpretation was correct.

With the receipt of this letter, the last barrier but
one before the execution of Mary had fallen. The final
barrier was Elizabeth herself. By now she probably
realized that there was no chance of saving Mary's life
when the whole nation was bent on her destruction.
But if she could not save her life, must she for ever
identify her own name with a queen's execution?
Might she not still salvage the honour of monarchy out
of a monarch's disaster? In such a mood Elizabeth
pinned her last hope to the Bond of Association.

Since, she pertinently asked, men had taken their
oaths to pursue Mary to the death, why did they now
hesitate to fulfil their undertaking? In other words,
why should not Mary be judicially murdered rather

than judicially executed? Clearly, if the Bond meant anything, it was the duty of the signatories to pursue Mary to the death *privately* without waiting for a warrant signed by the queen. The proposal had obvious political attractions. Majesty itself would not be debased to the level of common man, for Mary would be murdered, not executed. When attacked for the punishment of Mary by either James or the King of France, Elizabeth would be able to reply truthfully that it was not of her doing. She might indeed be tempted to go further, as a demonstration of her innocence, and arrest and execute the perpetrator of this desperate crime against Mary.

It was, of course, a piece of renaissance diplomacy, a game that men played all over Europe. But her ministers knew the techniques every bit as well as did Elizabeth, and they turned a deaf ear to her seductive appeal. They put the executioner's axe back in the hands of the queen. The last retreat from the importunate decision had been blocked. The death warrant, signed by the queen, was despatched to Fotheringay Castle; and, on February 8, 1587, with all the pomp appropriate to her personage, Mary, Queen of Scots was executed.

Like her grandson, Charles I, Mary went to her death with all the proud bearing of a martyr. What she had stood for all her life it is hard to say. She seems to have been carried along by the buffeting of events rather than by any dominating principles. She had succeeded to the Scottish throne as a child; had gone from the turbulence of Edinburgh to the sophistication of the French court; had returned to Scotland at the age of 18 as a widowed queen of France; and then had pursued a disastrous marital career ending in war and exile. Her blunders in Scotland as a queen had been followed by blunders in England as a prisoner. And in the end she had died for her errors no less than for her crimes. But if it was a life governed by no general and consistent principle, in the time of her death she found a cause, the Roman Catholic religion. Again like her grandson, nothing became her so well in the world as her manner of leaving it.

For once she outdid her cousin Queen Elizabeth in this display of honour. For the English queen was now faced with the impossible task of trying to justify the execution of Mary before a scandalized Europe. There was very little that could be done; but what little there was she did with every display of outraged monarchy. She wept, she went into mourning, she thundered abuse at her ministers. She forbad Burghley to come near the court. She announced to a scarcely credulous world that, although she had *signed* the execution warrant, she had withheld instructions for its delivery at Fotheringay, and that it had been sent off without her knowledge or permission. To prove it, she imprisoned in the Tower Davison, the Secretary of State in whose keeping the warrant had been. At the same time it became known that she was seriously considering the execution of one of her senior ministers for this dastardly crime against the Queen of Scots. Who could have been expected to believe this version of events it is impossible to say. How much credence Elizabeth herself attached to it is manifest by her continuing to pay Davison his salary while he was in the Tower, and releasing him when things quietened down.

In 1572, after the Ridolphi Plot, Parliament had called loudly for the execution of Mary, and only Elizabeth had shielded her. In 1586, after the Babington Plot, the parliamentary demand had been remorseless, with Elizabethan statesmen solidly in support. The ensuing months of indecision had once again seen the inner conflict between the heart and the mind. As ever in Elizabeth's case—and here the contrast with Mary, Queen of Scots is impressive—the mind conquered. It was as well. In personal terms, the death of Mary had in it all the solemn destiny of a Greek tragedy. In political terms, for Elizabeth—and England—there was no other course. It was essential as a preliminary to remove Mary, the crowned figurehead of internal opposition, if England was to enter confidently into the forthcoming battle for her national independence.

Chapter Nine

The Battle of England, 1588

T HE death of Mary, Queen of Scots removed a
serious obstacle to Queen Elizabeth. It performed
a similar service for Philip II of Spain. The Enterprise
of England had been brewing since at least 1585; but
he knew, of course, that its success would place Mary
—still bound to France by ties of family and tradition—on the English throne. He would thereby have
destroyed one enemy to strengthen another; unless, as
he may have guessed, the landing of the Armada forces
would have immediately cut short all introspective
arguments about the legality and procedures for trying Mary. The first Englishman to hand would have
cut off her head *sans trombone ni trompete*. But the
dilemma of having to choose, as it were, between Elizabeth and Mary was resolved for Philip by the execution
of Mary in February 1587. James VI of Scotland, in
English eyes, became the heir; but Philip and his allies,
including the pope, could claim that his heresy barred
him. Hence Philip had the opportunity now of conquest
as well as conversion.

The execution also finally resolved the dilemma of
English Catholics. Until then, the landing of Spanish
forces might have prompted the Catholics to stake all
in order to displace Elizabeth by Mary; but even this is

doubtful. After her death, to rise against Elizabeth to place either an heretical Scot or a Spanish princess on the English throne was hardly an inviting prospect. The execution of Mary proved, in fact, the last step towards the unification of England before the national threat from Spain. Away in Madrid and Rome and half a dozen other cities of refuge, English exiles warmed their chilled hopes with talk about thousands of their countrymen ready to rise against their queen at the first sound of Catholic gunfire. Cardinal Allen, their leader in Europe, drew up an elaborate plan of reform which the victorious Spanish forces should grant to England in the hour of their triumph. His paper plan went the way of the paper forces in England which he could create, supply and feed only from the hungry dreams of exile.

But if the Catholic exiles could only call upon an army of ghosts, Philip II had more substantial troops at his disposal. Both in the Netherlands and Spain he had battle-tested armies, as well as able commanders like the Duke of Parma and the Marquis of Santa Cruz. On the sea he had powerful galleons, heavy guns, skilful and experienced sailors, strong in their faith and confident in their mission. Against him, it is true, there would be seamen as battle-eager and inspired as any at his disposal, and among the motley collection of English warships and armed merchantmen would be examples of the most advanced naval architecture : fast ships with long-range guns. But many of the crews would be civilian sailors, called out only for critical times; and behind them, in England, there would be only a few veteran troops eked out with larger bodies of civilian soldiers. Yet like many of their brothers on the sea, what they lacked in battle experience they made up with the Protestant fire in their bellies. 'The battle will be bloody,' said a foreign observer, 'for the English never yield.'

Meanwhile, in spite of the considerable resources at their disposal, the Spanish commanders had mordant doubts about the feasibility of an amphibious operation against southern England. But, for once, Philip's irre-solution had gone; and in its place there was evolved an utterly preposterous piece of strategy begotten in the splendid isolation of his fortress-palace of the Escorial. A large task force of Spanish ships under Santa Cruz, carrying a considerable body of troops, would sail up-channel, join with Parma's waiting forces on the Netherlands coast, convoy them across to England, seize a southern port, pour men and supplies through it and inaugurate the conquest of England. To this end, as it became known during 1586, an Armada was col-lecting in Spanish ports.

This offensive strategy found as yet no echo in the mind of Elizabeth. But men like Sir Francis Drake at once grasped that the best plan to deal with the Armada was to destroy it before it sailed, while it lay at its assembly points along the Spanish coast. Only when the gravest warnings about Philip's intentions started to come through did Drake at last succeed in persuad-ing the queen to sponsor a bold defensive counter-

stroke. Ships were now collected from various sources
and placed under his command, with the whole project financed as a business venture (and the queen as a
considerable shareholder). It was given a double mission : first, to break up the Armada and, secondly,
pick up some part of the floating treasure fleet *en
route* to Spain from her empire. The second aspect of
Drake's venture would, it was hoped, pay for the first,
and yield also some reward to the shareholders.

At his Plymouth base Drake planned his enterprise
with secrecy and speed. Then, not a moment too soon,
he raced out of port for fear of a countermanding order
from the queen. Second thoughts did, in fact, produce
exactly such an order; but when her messenger reached
Plymouth he found no one there to receive it. Drake
made for Cadiz and, with his usual *élan*, rained blow
upon blow on the concentrated shipping and— no less
devastatingly—on Spanish morale. To describe the process as 'singeing His Catholic Majesty's beard' is a
characteristic English understatement for a bold and
brilliant measure. From a burning Cadiz, Drake sailed
along the coast of Spain, doing damage wherever he
could and searching, but this time in vain, to bring
some other part of the Armada to premature action.
Then, having picked up a handsome treasure ship, he
sailed for home.

Philip's Armada project had been damaged; but it
was not destroyed. Drake had forced delay upon him,
had won time for English preparations, had shown a
method for breaking the enemy in his home waters.

Repeated and enlarged, these measures might have torn the maritime initiative from Philip's hands and forced him altogether to abandon his schemes. But the months passed and Drake came no more.

For this the queen has been blamed. It is said that she starved her fleet and blunted its offensive spirit; kept it in port, paid off its crews and resumed her hopes for appeasement. But, within the narrow limits of government financial resources, what other policy lay open to her? Her successor, James I, once told the House of Commons that he would cut his suit according to his cloth. That extravagant monarch did nothing of the kind. But Elizabeth had sought such a happy solution all her life. 'Her Majesty did all by halves,' Sir Walter Ralegh would one day say of her. But, aware as she was of her heavy commitments and the close danger to the nation, it is hard to see that statesmanship would allow of any more adventurous policy than to tie up her ships and husband her resources. In the end she put home defence as the first priority of her military preparations. She kept Drake in Plymouth waiting for the Armada.

Meanwhile, in the severe battering which Drake had administered to Philip II, he had done even more damage than he thought. For the delays he imposed robbed Philip of his admiral, Santa Cruz. His death could not have come at a worse time for his master, who now proceeded to heap blunder on misfortune. To replace the senior commander in the middle of the preparations is hazardous enough. To replace him by someone like the Duke of Medina-Sidonia, who had little confidence either in himself as commander or in the plan of operations, invited trouble. And finally, to pin him down to a rigid strategic scheme, worked out in detail before hostilities began, courted disaster. 'If you fail, you fail,' the king told his reluctant admiral, 'but the cause being the cause of God you will not fail. Take heart and sail as soon as possible.' Having taken every reasonable step to ensure his own defeat, Philip II advanced to his destiny with the confident faith of a sleep-walker.

Elizabeth too, in keeping with tradition, chose an aristocrat for the supreme command, her kinsman, Lord Howard of Effingham. But he was a man who had a deep love for the sea and, combined with it, the marvellous capacity to take the units under his brilliant and highly individualistic subordinates and weld them into a coherent, loyal and flexible fighting machine. His *Ark Royal*—built for Ralegh's private purposes and, indeed, originally named the *Ark Ralegh* —was to become the ancestor of a famous line of ships. Under him, as vice-admiral, was Sir Francis Drake in the *Revenge*; as rear-admirals, in the *Triumph*, Sir Martin Frobisher, as turbulent as he was resourceful, and in the *Victory*, Sir John Hawkins, the sailor-administrator who had during recent years at the Navy Board fundamentally re-cast English naval strategy. And under them were the best Elizabethan captains, toughened in a hundred gales.

They probably had their equals among the Spaniards for, in spite of the misfortunes and blunders of Philip II, the fleet that he mobilized in the summer of 1588 was a large and powerful fighting force of brave men, able commanders and fine ships. Yet, it must be acknowledged, they lacked the advantage of fighting in known waters, with a friendly coast behind them. For them, the English channel was not a familiar line of communication but a running gauntlet of fire. They lacked also the naval genius of one like Drake who, in spite of rebuffs, was once more with irrepressible fervour pleading for authority to strike against the Spaniards before they left port.

Once again it looked for a moment as though Drake would be allowed to play his bold familiar hand. Once again an English fleet, this time under the supreme command of Howard of Effingham, set out for Spanish waters, having overcome the queen's innate resistance to adventures of this sort. But if the queen had swung round, so had the fickle wind. Blowing up from the south-west, it now favoured the Spaniards, not the English; and they turned round for home.

On July 12, 1588, the English fleet was back in Plymouth, baulked of its prey. On the 19th the Spaniards, at last on the move, were within sight of the Lizard; and, on instructions from Medina-Sidonia, they took up their predetermined battle order. For the moment the initiative lay with the Spaniards for, though long awaited, they had come sooner than expected. Initiative and surprise, combined with daring, might perhaps have given them a sharp victory: the capture of Plymouth and the destruction of a good part of the English

fleet in, or near port. But the occupation of Plymouth
was no part of Philip's strategy; and his admiral, not
daring to exploit his opportunity, pressed on to his appointed task. With brilliant manoeuvring the English
fleet turned the situation to its advantage, swung out
into the channel, pulled to the westward of the in-
vaders and, in so doing, called in the prevailing wind
as an ally.

The English were now *following* the Spaniards up-
channel, making vicious assaults on individual ships
but not seriously denting the main fleet, or indeed
effecting close contact with it. For, although the English ships, low built, fast moving, could swing hither
and thither to the pained embarrassment of the enemy,
the Spaniards carried very heavy guns which easily kept
the attackers at a respectful distance. Certainly it was
nothing of a pursuit but more like a procession, with the
stately Spanish formation shepherded carefully past the
south coast by an experienced and conscientious master
of ceremonies.

At last, with the Isle of Wight to the west of him—
his last prospect of an invasion base gone—the Spanish
commander looked for the happy juncture with the
troops of Parma, scheduled for the invasion and conquest of England. But Parma, himself blockaded by
Dutch ships, was in no position to comply; and, as the
Spanish fleet dropped anchor outside Calais, the whole
prefabricated strategy of Philip II came tumbling down
on the unfortunate head of his admiral. Now it was
Howard's chance to strike decisively. At midnight of

July 28 he let loose eight fireships, to be blown by the wind into the waiting fleet. To the nerve-tautened Spaniards, lying between their Dutch and English enemies, the strategem brought panic, familiar prologue to defeat. Without even waiting to heave anchor, they cut their cables and hastened out in disorder into mid-channel. The following day, in what has become known as the battle of Gravelines, Howard at last brought the enemy to combat and delivered some shattering—but by no means fatal—blows at the whole Armada. Probably four-fifths of the fleet was still intact, and a changing wind saved the Spaniards from being flung back on to the French coast.

But they had lost more than a battle, for their ammunition was gone; and their admiral, quite rightly, had no other thought but to seek the safest way home. Unfortunately the safest way was not also the shortest way. The Spanish visitors had lost all appetite for the channel trip, and Medina-Sidonia had therefore to make the terrible decision to strike *north* past England and up round Scotland and Ireland for home. Once again there was no pursuit but a procession, for both sides had run out of supplies; and before coming into Scottish waters the English, having seen the Spaniards off the premises, withdrew from the proceedings.

A decade before, Drake had won the imperishable glory of circumnavigating the globe. Now to the Spanish admiral there fell the lesser—and unsought— privilege of circumnavigating the British Isles. In unspeakable conditions of distress, hunger and disease, his shattered Armada plunged on, losing ships and men in the open sea, others by shipwreck on the Scottish coast. Still others sought haven on the Irish coast where, if any natives massacred their Spanish co-religionists, it was almost certainly under English orders. At length, the sadly broken fleet crawled home into port, to contradict the sweet rumours of victory, which had got there first, and to face the thankless obloquy of the Spanish nation.

Annus mirabilis? To Englishmen of those times, and long afterwards, this was the miraculous year. To this day, every schoolboy knows two dates : 1066, when England was conquered, and 1588, when she was not. This was the year when God blew—so a commemorative medal said—and the enemy was scattered. Forgetful of what had happened to the Huguenots of France on St Bartholomew's day, many Englishmen came to believe that the victory of 1588 was a sign of God's intervention on behalf of his Protestants.

The story of the Protestant wind has written itself so deeply into our folk memory that it calls at this stage for a brief comment. Certainly the veering wind on more than one occasion played havoc with the plans of the commanders. But that applied to both sides. In May 1588, when the Armada began to move, steady adverse winds delayed it and then a heavy gale damaged it. In the following month or two, by contrast, winds prevented three successive attempts of the English to reach Spain and repeat the 1587 exploit. On the other hand, the wind favoured the English for a time at Calais in blowing the fireships into the anchored Armada, but it deserted them soon after and saved the Armada from being wrecked on the north French coast. In trying to ascertain the causes of the English victory, it seems that we must eliminate the Protestant wind from our calculations. If there is any demonstrable quality about the wind during this period, it was governed by caprice, not dogma. The five crucial days of battle for the English channel may have formed part of a battle between the old faith and the new. If that was so, then the evidence seems to indicate that, while the guns thundered their religious discord, God was a neutral.

It is appropriate that we should remove the Protestant wind because it handicaps our assessment of the causes of victory. About these causes historians are now more or less agreed. The Spanish Armada was driven out of the English channel partly through its own errors, themselves stemming from the initial strategic blunder made in Spain. But it was defeated also by a fleet built according to more advanced concepts of maritime defence. English naval construction sacrificed tradition and superstructure to get a lighter, more manoeuvrable craft than the Spanish galleon. As a result, their ships could move with speed and freedom. To this they added better gunnery and generally superior naval skill. They could exploit an opportunity and, as at Plymouth, turn a dangerous situation into a favourable one. But like their enemies, they were soon short of supplies. Their skill and courage outdistanced their munitions.

To these causes of victory, we may perhaps add one

other, although it is difficult to assess it in precise terms.
But it may be that both sides, during the battle, reflected the social structure and whole outlook of the
contrasting nations they represented. If the battle was
finally won by initiative and flexibility, then these owed
something to the prevailing conditions of English
society, as compared with that of Spain. In England
there was little of the rigidity of the Spanish caste
system, of an articulated, hierarchical social order, or
of an exclusive and intolerant creed wholly victorious
in its battle against diversity. The English people, for
one reason or another, has always rejoiced in its diversity, and has always eluded any attempt to hammer it
into conformity. In the long run, the Elizabethan Act
of Uniformity was a failure: Catholic and Protestant
nonconformity alike have won their private wars
against a state church. Indeed, by 1588, there were
already unmistakable signs that, even in its limited
aims, the policy of uniformity was going to fail. Apart
from this, ultimate victory for nonconformity (which
meant later on liberty and individualism) was inherent
in the Elizabethan conception that the liberty of men's
souls was outside the range of government enquiry. By
now, it is true, in a dangerous political situation, Elizabeth was abandoning some of this flexibility. But it was
too late. And unity was preserved at the expense of
uniformity.

It is not without significance, therefore, that England's greatest victories have been won on the sea. Had
men been living during the last thirty years under Mary

Tudor instead of Elizabeth, there might have been a different story to tell. For uniformity might have won the day. But instead, thirty years of relative freedom had nurtured that individualism and flexibility so indispensable to men who fight against unpredictable winds and on unknown seas. The events of 1588 proved above all else that England's unity in diversity was a marvellous weapon for defence, as it was—in a later age—for conquest.

Because the Battle of the Channel was won, the Battle of England was, in one sense, not fought at all. Throughout the expectant summer of 1588 no inhabitant of England, except those who took to the sea, heard a single gun fired in anger. Plans were made—and came into operation as the beacon fires lit up southern England—for a *levée en masse*. In the counties the amateur armies, from the nobility right down to the peasantry, assumed their appointed duties. How these rustic soldiers would have acquitted themselves in battle it is impossible to speculate; but they clearly had another purpose as well. They were a demonstration to the world that England stood as an united nation under threat of the powerful forces of empire. In response to such a demonstration Elizabeth herself called upon all the Tudor sense of occasion and command.

Early in August she passed in review her army at Tilbury, as their general no less than their queen. The Armada was already broken as a fighting force, but Englishmen refused to believe that the danger had passed. It was as well; for it made possible the setting of one of the great moments of English history.

Elizabeth's Tilbury speech is indeed as famous in English literature as it is in English history. Every woman has in her the talents of an actress, but Elizabeth possessed them to a superb degree. To these she now added the greater talents of a statesman and a queen. The speech deserves to be recalled here since it displays the clear confidence of Elizabeth that the unity of England, which she had sought more than all else, stood at this time accomplished. With such a theme she addressed her troops, and through them the nation :

My loving people, we have been persuaded
By some that are careful of our safety
To take heed how we commit ourselves to armed
multitudes
For fear of treachery.

She scorned the advice.

Let tyrants fear.
I have always so behaved myself that, under God,
I have placed my chiefest strength and safeguard
In the loyal hearts and goodwill of my subjects.
And therefore I am come amongst you,
As you see at this time,
Not for my recreation and disport,
But being resolved, in the midst and heat of the battle,
To live or die amongst you all;
To lay down for my God,
And for my kingdom,
And for my people,

My honour and my blood
Even in the dust.
I know I have the body of a weak and feeble woman,
But I have the heart and stomach of a king,
And of a king of England too!
And think foul scorn that Parma or Spain,
Or any prince of Europe,
Should dare to invade the borders of my realm! ...

If we did not know that these words were written by Queen Elizabeth, we should be inclined to wonder whether they were written by William Shakespeare.

Chapter Ten

The Changing Pattern of Politics, 1589–95

'TRUTH it is,' Hakluyt had written in 1584, 'that through our long peace and seldom sickness (two singular blessings of Almighty God) we are grown more populous than ever heretofore.' The confident glow of his pages shines across the centuries; but he spoke too soon. Certainly, the population was growing, yet the process was slow, uneven and patchy. England was still a thinly populated country. But the 'long peace' was nearly over. The year 1584 was the last year before the opening of hostilities. And the time of 'seldom sickness' was passing too. England was entering on a period of unemployment, famine and plague. And, as the shadows lengthened, the queen found herself confronted with unfamiliar problems in an unfamiliar context.

By 1588 the Elizabethan system of government was thirty years old. At its pivot was the queen, established in the devotion of her subjects and secure in the headship of an united state. In Europe—even from her enemies—she had won a grudging respect. She had mastered the complex art of holding power, picked an able team of ministers, re-established and preserved the unity of England. She had governed patiently, economically and skilfully and, by the standards of the time, with humanity and tolerance.

Much undoubtedly had been achieved; and of this there would have been little without the unifying personality of the queen. It was only by her elevation above the bitter internal disputes, and by her assumption of some of the attributes of a goddess, that faction could be silenced and national policies, unpopular though they might be, pushed through. By now the divinity which hedged a crown was an acknowledged feature of the political scene.

These divine attributes had been fully exploited by Elizabeth in carrying through unpopular policies in the national interest, for example in diplomacy, her marriage and religion. But it was in religion that this assumption of divinity carried least conviction, especially among the Puritans. For, if the New Testament enjoined them to render unto Caesar the full rights of monarchy, the Old Testament had two whole books of Kings to remind them how sinful and mistaken kings might be. Peter Wentworth was deep in his devotion to Elizabeth; but he none the less felt it incumbent on him to remind her that princes might grievously err.

Until now the Puritans, while attacking the Elizabethan church settlement, had excluded Elizabeth personally from their attack. But a wider criticism was threatening. The bishops were under heavy fire and, in the ecclesiastical system, they were the last line of defence before the monarchy. If, therefore, Elizabeth began now to strike harshly at the critics, it is because she believed that she was fighting for monarchy itself. 'In the end,' Archbishop Whitgift once told Elizabeth, 'Your Majesty will find that those which now impugn the ecclesiastical jurisdiction [will] endeavour also to impair the temporal, and to bring even kings and princes under their censure.' Soon James VI, coming south to inherit the throne and the struggle, would put the issue more succinctly : 'No bishop, no king!' Less than fifty years after the death of Elizabeth the Puritans would pronounce the same thing to Archbishop Laud *and* Charles I—with the help of an axe. Whatever happened to Calvinistic puritanism in practice, in theory it was democratic; and, as in Geneva, it could get on perfectly well without the services of a monarch.

In England Calvinists were already addressing the queen's highest ministers as though they were merely sinful members of God's Church. We may take as an example the report by Henry Barrow, one of the fathers of Congregationalism, of his examination before members of the Privy Council, including the Archbishop of Canterbury, the Bishop of London, the Lord Chancellor and the Lord Treasurer :

> *Lord Treasurer [Burghley] said: 'Why are you in prison?'*
> *Barrow: 'I am now in prison, my Lord, upon the statute made for recusants.'*
> *Lord Treasurer: 'Why will you not come to the church?'*

Barrow: 'My whole desire is to come to the church of God.'

Lord Treasurer: 'Thou art a fantastical fellow, I perceive, but why not to our churches?'

Barrow: 'The causes are many and great, my Lord, and it were too long to show them in particular. But briefly, my Lord, I cannot come to your churches because all the wicked and profane of the land are received into the body of your churches. Again, you have a false and anti-Christian ministry set over your churches, neither worship you God aright, but after an idolatrous and superstitious manner. And your church is not governed by the word of God but by Romish courts.'

Lord Treasurer: 'Indeed, I perceive you have a delight to be an author of this new religion.'

At this , the Lord Chancellor interposed to say that 'he never heard such stuff in all his life'.

After such relatively polite beginnings Barrow finished up by describing the archbishop (Whitgift) to his face as 'a monster, a miserable compound, I know not what to call him. He is neither ecclesiastical nor civil.' He added that he was 'the second beast that is spoken of in the Revelation'. Burghley, who cordially disliked Whitgift, added salt to the wound by asking Barrow to give him the reference for the quotation; to which he replied: 'The thirteenth chapter of Revelations, verse eleven,' and was promptly dragged from the room by his guard.

This was an open attack on Whitgift—Elizabeth's 'little black husband' as she called him—the man who, in these later years, came in religious matters nearer to

Elizabeth's way of thinking than did any of her ministers. Burghley, who in so much else stood closest to the queen, was shocked by Whitgift's tough anti-Puritan policy, which he had introduced on becoming archbishop in 1583. 'By chance,' Burghley once wrote to him : 'I am come to the sight of an instrument [issued from Lambeth Palace] of twenty-four articles, of great length and curiosity, found in a Romish style, to examine all manner of ministers in this time . . . which I have read, and find so curiously penned, so full of branches and circumstances, as I think the inquisitors of Spain use not so many questions to comprehend and to trap their preys.' It is not surprising that Burghley has been called a Puritan sympathizer. 'My Lord,' said Whitgift, 'an old friend is better than a new; and I trust Your Lordship will not so lightly cut off your old friends for any of these new-fangled and factious sectaries.'

Burghley was no Puritan. But, as a statesman, he saw the danger of driving the Puritans, and therefore their parliamentary allies, too far. Yet it may be that, in the political conditions of the day, Whitgift and the queen were right and Burghley wrong. But it was fortunate for the Church of England that, if it bred a truculent disciplinarian like Whitgift, it also bred the cautious statesman like Burghley, and the gentle and judicious Richard Hooker, who fought against the dangers of Puritan intransigence without himself employing the dark weapons of intolerance.

But if men like Barrow attacked the queen's ministers

THE CHANGING PATTERN 163

rather than the queen, John Penry, 'a poor young man, born and bred in the mountains of Wales', as he described himself, was driven to carry the argument to its logical conclusion. At first his attack had been oblique, implying that the queen's policy was being carried through against the queen's will, and could not really represent her true faith. But, he pointed out, her policy would be damaging to her memory.—'For what will our children that rise after us and their children say, when they shall be brought up in gross superstition, but that it was not Queen Elizabeth's will that we their parents should have that true religion she professed made known unto us? Will not the enemies of God's truth with unclean mouths avouch that she had little regard unto true or false religion any further than it belonged unto her profit?' The queen, he declared, had a duty to introduce the true religion, under guidance from God. But, he added ominously, 'If one will not do it, He can find another whom He will honour with the deed.' 'Oh, Queen Elizabeth,' he once cried, 'spare the Church of God, and know yourself to be but mortal woman!'

Mortal woman she may have been, but she was also head of a Church faced with a most deadly onslaught. For the bishops, her servants, were now under devastating attack from the virulent pen of 'Martin Marprelate'. Who Martin was the government never discovered; nor have historians. He may have been John Penry himself, or Job Throckmorton, the Puritan M.P., or Sir Roger Williams (the original of Shakespeare's

Fluellen); or all three, or none. Certainly, he was a coarse and brilliant controversialist who raked the bench of bishops with his murderous fire. The pamphlet war opened with the *Epistle,* issued in November 1588 : '. . .But you see my worshipful priests of this crew, to whom I write, what a perilous fellow M. Marprelate is. He understands of all your knavery, and it may be he keeps a register of them. Unless you amend, they shall all come into the light one day.'

There followed half a dozen scurrilous tracts, savagely lampooning the bishops and their friends. As they grew in ferocity some of the moderate supporters of reform may well have been driven into the opposite camp. But before the full revulsion could set in, the government had tracked down the itinerant printing press and scattered the organization behind it. The whole thing was over in a year, but it had kept half England amused, and it had landed some memorable blows on the bishops and, by inference, upon the head of their order, the queen herself. To her these activities carried the same marks of treason as did the efforts of the Jesuits; and they called for the same treatment. Barrow and his colleague Greenwood were hanged in 1593 for treason. So was Penry, in the same year. Others died in prison. As compared with the Catholics, the number of Protestant martyrs was small. But to their allies in the House of Commons it was a gloomy augury of a betrayed Church.

It has sometimes been said that Puritanism at this stage consisted of a radical movement of young men against the entrenched conservatism of elderly bishops. Some of the leaders undoubtedly were young men : Penry had crowded much into his life but he was still only 30 at the time of his execution. It is true, also, that many of the early radicals, in advancing to the middle years of their lives, had been lost beyond recall. But many remained; and of these the greatest was that doughty old warrior, Peter Wentworth who, in this year of trial, 1593, decided to make his last stand for a defeated cause. But this time it was not to be for the Puritan prayer book or organization, but for something which was more intimate and fundamental to the queen herself.

The problem of her marriage was, of course, no longer a live issue. But in its place there was another which grew more acute with each passing year. Thanks to the marriage policies of the Tudors and their predecessors, there were a number of claimants to the succession, some quite absurd, others with a fighting chance of success—if they could persuade anyone to fight for them. Most responsible Englishmen, however, believed that James VI of Scotland was the only suitable candidate for the throne. But the queen, who all her life had resisted any proposal formally to nominate her successor, was as adamant on the subject at 60 as she had been at 30. That was her principle and she held fast to it. Hence no English statesman was allowed, in any overt way, to acknowledge or declare the queen's successor.

Peter Wentworth had no hesitation in rushing in

where statesmen feared to tread. Hence he arrived at the 1593 Parliament with a speech ready, and with it a draft Act setting out the succession. He had also worked out the subsequent measures for putting pressure on the queen. So equipped, he rallied his old Puritan allies and gave them advance notice of his plan. To his pained surprise he found them slow to respond. Perhaps they had been more fortunate than Wentworth : for time had taught them prudence. They saw that a parliamentary bill of this nature was an open threat to the prerogative and would run up against the fierce, and still powerful, resistance of the queen. Wentworth was unmoved; and he went on looking for an influential group of members who, when the time came, would back his speech.

But the speech was, in the end, not delivered. For news of the plan had reached the Privy Council which promptly placed Wentworth in the Tower. There he remained until his death four years later—faithful in his seventies as ever he was to the idea of freedom of speech, refusing to retract, he said, even if he were offered a dukedom and £20,000 a year. Undoubtedly the queen regarded him as a danger for, right at the end of his life, when he longed for a breath of country air, she felt that she could not spare him even that. So he died as he had lived, the faithful champion of all the lost causes of Elizabethan England.

In one respect it is a pity that Wentworth's speech was not delivered, for the debate might have been one of the most revealing ever held in an Elizabethan House of Commons. The bill would, of course, have been frustrated, but the discussion would have illumined some of the dark corners of Elizabethan constitutional thinking.

We lack the evidence; but elsewhere in this parliament there is enough to show the stiffening resistance of both the queen and some of her Commons. James Morrice, a stalwart Puritan who parted company with Wentworth on the succession bill, launched out separately in a bold assault on the whole ecclesiastical policy of Whitgift which, he declared, menaced all men's liberty. Shall we, he cried, '. . . yield our bodies to be burned, our consciences to be ransacked, and our inheritance to be disposed at the pleasure of our prelates, and not so much as once open our mouths to the contrary?' To this rhetorical question the queen supplied some very short answers, namely a period of restraint for Morrice, his dismissal from the important office of Attorney of the Court of Wards, and a declaration, through the Speaker of the House of Commons, 'commanding expressly that they should not intermeddle at all with any other matter of state or touching causes ecclesiastical'. The Speaker was charged, as he said, on his allegiance, 'that if any bill should be preferred touching these two points I should not suffer it to be read'.

The late embers of the smouldering Puritan fires were heavily stamped down. Morrice, like Wentworth, had fought his last battle : before the end of 1597 both men were dead. But, for the queen, there were other

battles to be fought : and this time without the pro-
tective umbrella of her prerogative. A fundamental
constitutional debate would begin in these years and
would turn on her need for money which was by now
very acute, for she was more deeply involved in war.
These were wars in the national interest : all the con-
fusing campaigns were made coherent as a bitter
struggle with Spain fought on a wide front. But many
members of the House of Commons, when it came to
raising funds, seemed to believe that the battles could
be fought to a large extent at the private charge of the
queen. To her growing needs, even five short years after
the Armada, they responded with tight lips and purses.

We should not, of course, dismiss this attitude as the
mean responses of hard-faced men. They saw that,
if national security was deeply involved, other important interests were also at stake. In issues of the prerogative they had always been blocked. But in taxation
the initiative lay with them. Here then was another
method by which they might perhaps breach the prerogative, gain a voice in 'matters of state'. They tried, as
before, to make their grants conditional grants, that is,
on condition that government took account of their
political views. They had therefore, as an essential preliminary, to make it clear that they alone determined
taxation, not the queen or the House of Lords. Taxation
always has been in English history the thin end of the
constitutional wedge. By means of it the Commons
would again and again press their claim for a voice in
government until at last, long afterwards, they won it.

Francis Bacon, whose ambiguous career is for a moment illumined in this 1593 debate by a bold expression of his views, spoke clearly. So did a lesser M.P. who cut out from the preamble to the subsidy act the words 'prostrating ourselves, our lives and lands at Her Majesty's feet'. So did the Puritan Robert Beale. So did a number of others. After vehement discussion the result was a compromise. The queen got her taxation, though less warmly and less speedily than her necessities required. It was a token of the times : an experiment in constitutional manoeuvre which, under the Stuarts, would be developed much further until by means of it government at last would be brought to a standstill.

In the early 1590s the Elizabethan system began to show signs of strain. The relatively stable conditions of peace, upon which it had been erected, were gone. The queen was committed to war in the Netherlands. Now, with the assassination of Henry III, the last of Catharine de Medici's sons, the Valois line was extinguished; and she was committed therefore to France also. Her ally, the Protestant Henry of Navarre was now king, in name if not in power; but he would have to fight—as well as be converted to Catholicism—for his capital. His greatest opponent was Philip II, making large efforts to turn France into a Spanish satellite. If Elizabeth opposed Spain in the Netherlands she would have to oppose it also in France, with substantial aid in money and men. She would have to go on fighting Spain on the high seas as well, losing some of her best captains and finest ships in the process. She would have to carry on an exhausting struggle in Ireland, a relent-less, unrewarding war of attrition which would swallow up a whole fortune without trace.

Now the queen was forced to do increasingly what she had resisted doing all her life. She had to seek large parliamentary grants; and, since these were inade-quate, to exploit more intensively non-parliamentary sources : the feudal dues, monopolies and the rest. But, forced as she was to go in search of unpopular devices, she thereby prepared for herself a growing volume of parliamentary criticism. That criticism came from the very people who met her urgent needs with minimal taxation, and therefore forced her to resort to such de-testable methods. So, while Parliament continued to display all the outward show of devotion, it became in effect doggedly hostile to her fiscal aims; and it tried, with some success, to seize the initiative in the field of economic policy. It remained for the great parliamen-tary debate of 1601 to show how little of the early Elizabethan financial system remained.

Equally subject to change was the whole govern-mental order. The long partnership between Elizabeth and Burghley was drawing to a close. He was already in his middle seventies, but he continued to show flashes of the old industry, and was always capable of shrewd counsel. Still, everybody knew that his time was run-ning out; and the claimants to his power were already disputing over the inheritance. Robert Cecil, his son, was in his early thirties, but he already had the experienced hand of an administrator. Robert Devereux, Earl of Essex, a few years younger, was a more attractive man, a soldier-courtier of gallantry and charm, and with a special place in the affections of the queen. To one or other, power might pass in the last years of the queen. But a general share out of office could be expected: and able men like Sir Walter Ralegh, Sir Francis Bacon, Sir Edward Coke and many others were already jostling for position. In this struggle there was always the danger that the queen herself might have to fight to retain the dominant role she had held for forty years. It was one of the tragedies of the last decade of her reign that she had to face one of her greatest crises so late in the day, and alone.

Here were the warnings of grave questions of state whose answers could not much longer be delayed. But the queen had never liked crossing her bridges before she reached them. In any case she was still strong in the affections of her people; and, on her summer progresses, the new generation displayed the same warmth and delight in her presence as their fathers and grandfathers had done before them. She had always made these tours and had shown amazing stamina and resilience amid the strenuous journeys, the *longueurs* of ornate pageantry, the elaborate masques and the stylized effusions of the versifiers.

Here, too, she resembled Philip II who, when called upon, could long endure the untiring devotions of his subjects. In 1592, for example, when visiting the

English Jesuit College at Valladolid he faced addresses
of welcome and praise—in verse—spoken by ten
students respectively in Hebrew, Greek, Latin, English,
Scots, Welsh, Spanish, French, Italian and Flemish!
Elizabeth would, on her visits to the universities, sit
through hours of adulatory verse, theatrical performance and theological disputation without any serious
show of fatigue. Once, it is true, at Oxford, growing
weary of the complex oration of a theologian (a
former Professor of Divinity in the University), she sent
him a message to cut it short. It had no effect. She
thereupon sent him another, with the same result.
Viewed from one angle it might look as though the
orator was here offering a bold defence of academic
liberty against the opposition of an intruding monarch.
In fact it was nothing of the kind. It was subsequently
learned that the speaker felt that he could not modify
his elaborate, carefully prepared oration in any way
without ruining the whole affair. Having started he
could not stop; he must go on to the end. So the queen's
failure is merely one more piece of evidence that it is
quite impossible to stem the timeless eloquence of a don.

But she had other ways of teaching him a lesson. The
following day she herself made a Latin oration. Half-
way through she noticed that Lord Burghley, though
lame with gout, was obliged to stand. She at once interrupted her speech to demand a stool for him; and,
only when it came, did she resume. The assembly took
the interlude to be, not only a public tribute to the old

Lord Treasurer, but a rebuke to the orator of the previous day who had failed to extricate himself from the tight clutches of his own speech.

One of the most memorable events of her later progresses was the entertainment arranged for her in September 1591 (the year before she went to Oxford) at Elvetham in Hampshire, the home of the Earl of Hertford. Here were staged colourful masques; water sports, complete with sea nymphs, gods and goddesses; feasts, music, dancing, games, fireworks. For four whole days the queen threw herself energetically into the festivities, and she was as fresh and gay at the end as at the beginning, delighting in every moment of this impressive display of her subjects' devotion and loyalty.

Only the weather was fickle: now bright, now stormy. And, finally, at the queen's departure from Elvetham Park, for which a splendid farewell ceremony had been arranged, the heavens opened and poured torrents of rain remorselessly down upon the queen and performer alike. Still the ceremony went on as arranged, the dripping actors reciting their verses as they stood in the sodden grass. As a result, the lament of the country poet, which had been designed as a moving allegory on the departing goddess, became as well a factual description of a September day in the English countryside:

> O see, sweet Cynthia, how the watery gods,
> Which joyed of late to view thy glorious beams,
> At this retire do wail and wring their hands
> Distilling from their eyes salt showers of tears.

Perhaps the queen saw also in his verses a grave symbolism deeper than his words:

Leaves fall, grass dies, beasts of the wood hang head.
Birds cease to sing and every creature wails
To see the season alter with this change;
For how can summer stay when sun departs?

For the queen, too, it was the beginning of autumn.

Chapter Eleven

Disenchantment, 1596—1603

SO far, English unity had held fast: in peace, in the long years of religious discord and international insecurity, and in the severe test of battle in the English channel. The question facing Elizabeth in the late 1590s was: would English unity also hold during the wearing years of costly stalemate?

Certainly, although she could still be gay and energetic, she was beginning to feel within herself the passage of the years. This is nowhere better revealed than in a contemporary account that we possess of her swearing in of Sir Thomas Egerton as Lord Keeper of the Great Seal, on May 6, 1596.[1] The queen was dressed from head to toe in a straw-coloured gown of satin, all richly decorated with silver, with hat adorned with pearls, and shoes to match. She stood on a Turkey carpet, under the cloth of estate, and before her on a table lay the Great Seal with its red velvet purse and leather bag. Beside her was Lord Burghley, Lord High Treasurer, 'who was licensed to sit on a stool with his back toward the arras by reason of his indisposition and weakness'. There, in her privy chamber, in the presence of her great officers of state, she handed Egerton his seal and directed him to his duty. On his knee he

[1] I am indebted to Dr. W. J. Jones for the reference.

humbly thanked her, at the same time declaring his
unworthiness; whereupon the queen placed her hands
on his shoulders as though to raise him up—a formal
gesture to show that she had taken him into her service.

Then, when the ceremony was complete, she allowed
herself for a moment to look back over the years. She
told him of her first lord keeper, Sir Nicholas Bacon—
'and he was a wise man, I tell you'—and then added
that she knew that Egerton would be her last. Ever
tactful, Burghley at once interjected: 'God forbid,
Madam! I hope you shall bury four or five more.' 'No!'
replied the queen, 'this is the last'; and 'clapping her
hand on her heart' she wept for a while, and then
hurried from the chamber.

The queen's forecast proved better than Lord Burghley's: she had no more lord keepers. But she still had
immense reserves of energy, and could call upon them
from time to time with devastating effect. A year later,
for example, she gave a display of Tudor fire which
would have done credit to any monarch in the time of
his greatness.

A Polish ambassador arrived in London in July
1597. Because the queen knew and respected his father,
she varied the established procedure, under which dip-
lomats presented their credentials to the Privy Council,
and decided to receive him personally, in the presence
of her courtiers. This warm gesture was met with a
rebuff. The ambassador, having kissed the hand of the
queen, then drew back a few yards in order to make a
bellicose oration in Latin, attacking the queen's treat-

ment of Polish neutrals while she was engaged in hostilities with Spain, and threatening war. In choosing so public an occasion for so menacing a speech, he stung the queen into a brilliant display of extempore oratory. 'Exspectavi legationem:' she thundered, 'mihi vero querelam adduxisti.' [I awaited an embassy: what you have brought me is an accusation.] Then, continuing in Latin throughout, she gave him a thorough trouncing, mingling contempt with irony, but assuring him none the less that, if he had a just complaint, it would be freely heard. Then, when it was all over, she could not resist a display of her delicious sense of anticlimax. Changing from Latin to English, she murmured for the benefit of her assembled courtiers: 'God's death, My Lords . . . I have been enforced this day to scour up my old Latin that hath lain long in rusting.'

We owe this account of a famous scene to Sir Robert Cecil who, prompted by the queen, sent a description of it to the Earl of Essex.

Between these two ambitious young men, Cecil and Essex, relations were still outwardly friendly; but the rupture was not far distant. Within four years the one would be at the centre of power and the other dead; and all this was a sequel to the death of Lord Burghley on August 4, 1598. At once the problem of finding his successor—the latent crisis, present for a decade—thrust itself ineluctably on the queen. That she must now think of new men was sadly manifest to her. That she must also think of new policies she could not—or would not—acknowledge.

Burghley had been a great statesman : of that there can be no doubt. His capacity for work was enormous. Even to this day the historian is puzzled by his immense output of letters, memoranda, directives, many of them written in his own forceful, angular hand. Most of his work was done in the shadows of greatness : and it suited his temperament. For fame and the applause of listening senates he had little taste. He loved power and wielded it to the last; but the panoply of power did not captivate him. He would rather be a servant in his mistress's house—at least that is the impression we get —than sit in the seat of the mighty. It suited him as well as his mistress that the cult of personality should flourish. But it was not *his* personality : and the cult of Gloriana obscures, perhaps for ever, a good deal of what we should like to know.

Like his queen, he assimilated without difficulty the lessons of renaissance politics and proved a skilled practitioner in the art. He could be sly, unscrupulous and, if the interests of the state required it, remorseless, as he became in the end to Mary, Queen of Scots. It is true, also, that some of his immense labour was spent in the service of his family, but a good deal more was spent in the unselfish service of his country. He gladly devoted long hours of a long life to mastering the joyless details of government finance and administration. He gave to his queen the untiring service of a conservative, and his policy echoed and reinforced the powerful convictions of the queen.

In that same year another great conservative died;

one who had carried heavier burdens of government even longer than the forty years of Burghley and his queen. Philip II of Spain, to our insular eyes, lacks the stature of even modest greatness. To us he is the great failure : the man who set out to destroy England but in fact succeeded only in destroying half his own grand fleet. But such a judgement misses something of the pathetic grandeur of the man : his unremitting hard work to hold together a mosaic empire which stretched from the Low Countries through Spain and Portugal out into the new world. He failed against England; he failed in the Netherlands. But in all else he held firm and passed on intact, nay, vastly extended, a prodigious inheritance to his son. If this was achieved, in part, by extinguishing Spanish diversity and imprisoning the Spanish soul in a straitjacket of uniformity, he was merely conserving the established Spanish tradition.

'If we are to choose', wrote the Spanish historian, Menendez y Pelayo, 'between the maritime greatness of England under her Virgin Queen, and the slow martyrdom and impoverishment of our own nation, which during two centuries was the unselfish arm of the Church, no heart that beats with enthusiasm for the noble and the beautiful will hesitate to bestow the palm on us.' There may be some doubt as to whether Philip's policy was as much a policy of the 'unselfish arm of the Church' as we have sometimes been led to believe; at least one pope did not think it was. But of Philip's abiding resolution for the uniformity of Spain, there can be no question. If that could only be achieved at the cost ultimately of greatness and liberty, many Spaniards gladly paid the price. The English preference for unity and liberty at the expense of uniformity belongs to a different tradition.

Of the three conservatives who had played so large a part in sixteenth-century Europe, only one remained : the queen herself. Now as she looked back, alone, over four decades of government, she might well have been pardoned for taking pride in her achievement. She had brought unity and strength to a divided England. She had met threats at home with courage and from abroad with defiance. She had inspired admiration among her people and victory on the high seas. She would leave England within striking distance of the time of her imperial greatness.

How had this been achieved? The answer to this question is not to be found in some fundamentally new concept of government, evolved by the Tudors and carried through by their ministers. None of the Tudors had the capacity or desire for fundamental or original political thinking. Henry VII, Henry VIII and Elizabeth each possessed the skill for discovering, adapting and exploiting useful machinery of government and endorsing it with the personal qualities of their dynasty. They looked to the past; and even when one of them, Henry VIII, made a revolution, it was an eclectic, ramshackle compromise embracing much more of the old than the new. Like her ancestors, Elizabeth I was not a political philosopher but a pragmatic monarch.

Here there is a sharp contrast between the last Tudor

and the first Stuart. When James I came south in 1603, to succeed Elizabeth, he carried in his baggage weighty chapters of political thought, composed by himself, which contained in them enough explosive material to sink a ship. Queen Elizabeth, by contrast, preferred to travel light. She held strong views about the princely prerogative, about the limited role of Parliament, about her governing powers in the Church and her social responsibility for her subjects. But she expounded no philosophical system of government. *Solvitur ambulando* might well have been her motto. She preferred to wait on events.

But if there was no rigorous system of political doctrines by which she ruled, she could achieve her aims by other means. Her solution in fact lay in so elevating the queen above the rest of mankind that policies in the national interest would—along with her personality—pass out of reach of human criticism. In an age when forceful minorities pressed for extreme measures, she could, as in the case of religion, damp down harsh passions, identify her own person with a moderate national Church, and hope that time would confirm her compromise. It was a technique, rather than a philosophy, of government; and she would use it over and over again. As the reign proceeds we are witnessing, in the fields of politics as in literature, the apotheosis of a woman, a monarch transmuted into a god.

It was not the last time that this would happen in English history. The same development would occur under Charles I, but it would be used in a different way and to a different end. That monarch came to believe with an intense passion in the divinity of kings, in their peculiar access to divine guidance, and in their immunity to the demands and criticisms of mortal men. In his last years he passed wholly out of reach of the arguments of the Puritan opposition. This royal mood was expressed in politics but it was reinforced in art. The portraits which Van Dyck made of him confirmed and intensified the sanctity of his royal mission to preserve intact the Stuart kingship. It is hard, in this case, to distinguish cause from effect; but certainly the Van Dyck portraits conveyed to Charles—as did also the Rubens paintings of his father in Whitehall Palace— the unapproachable divinity of the kingly calling.

In Elizabethan England there were few great painters; but it saw the emergence of a vast popular literature, a good deal of which focused itself upon the queen. This cult, unfortunately, has never been properly investigated. When it is, it will no doubt call for other approaches besides that of the historian. Ultimately a study of this kind may well open up a new vision of Elizabethan government and society.

This is not to say that Elizabeth invented the cult; nor that it was invented and fostered by any particular group of men; nor that the adulation in which Elizabeth basked was insincere. What, however, can be said is that, in this process of deification, Elizabeth found to hand a political instrument of immense power, subtlety and range, and that she used it with consummate skill, wisdom, courage and ingenuity.

By means of it the nation was kept unified when it might easily have splintered into a series of discordant religious sects. By calling upon it the queen could insulate her ideals for the unity of England, and the power of the monarchy, against the unyielding questions of the hour. Believing in it, Englishmen brought a powerful enemy to battle and tore victory from him when prudence would have sounded retreat. Inspired by it, Englishmen wrote some of the finest passages in their great literature.

But it should not be forgotten that it was an instrument *ad interim*, an instrument of provisional value and limited life. And instruments, if used over too long a period, tend to wear out. The cult of personality could not, as such, supply answers to a single one of the pressing political issues of the time. Instead, it tended in the end to decline into a series of political clichés, decked out with some elaborate love-tricks of which the queen was the supreme executant. In the first thirty years this elevation of the queen served the nation well. In the last years of her reign it postponed the solution of urgent problems. It may have done more harm than good.

A little while after her death, Sir Walter Ralegh— that brilliant political analyst who was such a failure in the game of politics—said of Elizabeth that she was 'a lady whom time had surprised'. It was a cruel and bitter epigram by a bitter man who, during the grey years of disappointment, had eaten his heart out as he watched second-rate men climb to advancement above him. But the epigram enshrines a truth. Old age does not usually develop new virtues or vices in us. Rather, it tends to accentuate some of those that we already possess. So it was with Queen Elizabeth and her great minister, Lord Burghley. Old age, though expected, had indeed taken them by surprise; and, as their innate conservatism took full control, they stared in bewilderment at a changing situation. Elizabeth, all her life, made shrewd decisions, but she had also found that in some circumstances only vacillation, ambiguity and conservatism would serve. If these did not always add up to a policy, they could at least be dressed up to look like one. Sometimes her solutions were hardly more than a miscellaneous collection of devices. Sometimes they were far-sighted, as well as enriched by the high idealism of the queen and her subjects. On the whole they had served her and her people well; and she believed in them. Hence it became impossible, at the last, to adopt new and untried policies.

But, unfortunately, it was new policies that were required for, although the queen was not changing, the times were. It was unfortunate also that, in the last decade of her life, England was passing through a severe economic depression which her ministers met with the ideas and methods of their grandfathers.

From 1594, for three years in succession, the summer rainfall was extremely heavy. Each autumn the green corn yielded a scanty harvest. For three years in succession famine ravaged the land, especially in the midland counties. In Oxfordshire, at last, in 1596 the starving peasantry rose in arms. Not for the last time in our history, the nation blamed the government when it might have blamed the weather. It was also peculiarly unlucky for Elizabeth that, in 1597, the purchasing power of wages fell lower than perhaps at any time between the thirteenth century and the present day.

In that year, a thoroughly alarmed government bethought itself of an ancient remedy and put through Parliament a new act against enclosure. Fifty years before, such an act might have brought succour, though even that is doubtful. But now it was out of time and offered nothing but the illusory prospect of relief. In industry also, hamstrung by the distortions of monopoly we have, as in agriculture, a chronicle of failure : a government running out of ideas.

The same was true of the succession problem. While Mary, Queen of Scots, was alive, Elizabeth quite rightly refused to name her successor. For, if she named Mary, many of her Protestant subjects would have taken alarm at the prospect—and taken steps to prevent it. If Elizabeth had endorsed some other claimant, then she would have aroused Scottish hostility, broken the Scottish alliance and faced other trouble as well. But after 1587 Mary, Queen of Scots was dead. The heir was her son, James VI, an undoubted Protestant, who would do nothing to alienate Elizabeth by stirring up rebellion, as had been shown in 1587. To name him as successor would have been welcome to many in both

England and Scotland. Yet Elizabeth never named him : the story that she did so on her deathbed rests on somewhat slender evidence. But because she did not name him, her own ministers, like Robert Cecil, anxious to establish a smooth succession had, towards the end of her reign, to communicate with James in code behind the queen's back. Here is a sample of their correspondence :

> . . . *the suspicion or disgracing of 10 [Cecil] shall touch 30 [James] as near as 10; and when it shall please God that 30 shall succeed to his right, he shall no surelier succeed to the place than he shall succeed in bestowing as great and greater favour upon 10 as his predecessor doth bestow on him.*

In short, Cecil was being guaranteed security of tenure when the business of government changed hands.

But ministers who conducted a secret correspondence with a foreign monarch made themselves liable, in some circumstances, to a charge of treason. In addition, the whole situation encouraged a lot of backstairs dealing with James and led to the denigration of one minister by another in his eyes. This was an example of the queen using an out-of-date policy when the circumstances had changed. But here policy was supported by pride. She hated to think of anyone taking her place. It must have been like the sound of footsteps walking over her tomb.

The real test of Elizabethan statesmanship came indeed in the very last years of her reign for, in 1601, all the unresolved issues of the period, in Court and Parliament, came to a head. At Court they were focused on the Earl of Essex, the last of Queen Elizabeth's favourites.

Essex personified some of the most enviable qualities in an Elizabethan aristocrat. He was handsome, gallant, a brave and humane soldier. At the age of 20 he won fame at Zutphen; and with one courageous exploit after another he climbed ever higher in the esteem of the nation and in the affection of the queen. It would, of course, be fantastic to argue that there was any love affair, in the accepted sense, between this picturesque soldier and his aging queen. Their relationship belonged rather to the elaborate, romantic façade of the high Elizabethan governing class. Within the pseudo-romance of a courtship, the virgin queen retained to the end the role of eagerly sought—but never conquered —maiden. Behind the façade, large political issues were fought out among the queen's ministers, and throughout the period there was a fierce, unrelenting struggle for power. Everything was, in fact, conducted on two levels : in the adorned language of amorous devotion, and beneath it in the sharp cut-and-thrust for office and power, in which the queen held the unbreached authority to decide. Every one of her gallant courtiers clenched the mailed fist beneath the velvet glove.

Essex was no different from the rest. But he made the fatal mistake of treating the façade as though it were the reality. Possessing, as he did in *excelsis*, the courtier's talents of gallantry and charm, he believed that by these he could override the acknowledged processes of

Elizabethan political behaviour. Under the queen's
system, no single man could be supreme, or could con-
centrate in himself any monopoly of power. There
were no mayors in the Elizabethan palace. Rivalry and
faction went from top to bottom in the state. The queen
knew that it was essential to divide if she was to rule.
But Essex, impatient, quarrelsome, swinging wildly
between over-confidence and despair, wanted more
than this. He hoped that, in gaining a peculiar place in
the queen's affections, he would win a dominant voice
in the queen's government. He broke the rules of the
game.

Certainly he could, in the sunset of the reign, give
the queen the sweet illusions of a courtship with none of
its attendant risks. There was undoubtedly, on her part,
an emotional response to him; but it was carefully cir-
cumscribed within the time-hardened barriers of her
statecraft. These barriers Essex under-estimated. But if
he thereby misjudged the queen, she did not misjudge
him. She judged him worthy of her friendship and
bounty but incapable, as yet, of the highest office. In
any case, she would always deny him sole and supreme
power. She was determined that the system must be
maintained as before, and the political game played
according to her long-established rules.

At last Essex recognized the situation for what it was.
At each attempt to place his followers in key offices the
queen said no. When he tried to win senior office for
himself, as master of the Court of Wards, again the
queen said no. This high-spirited, tempestuous young

man had drunk deeply from every cup of disappointment that the Elizabethan state had to offer him. Heavily in debt, disillusioned, Essex at last committed an act
of political suicide. He begged for service in Ireland,
graveyard of so many English reputations. Once there,
he re-enacted the misfortunes of his predecessors, including his own father, who had gone there twenty-
five years before. He fought campaigns without issue
and made negotiations without peace. Having reaped
a bitter harvest, he returned without authority to England; and from now on he slid at a growing pace from
blunder into treason. Thwarted at every turn, he struck
back with a frontal assault against the whole Elizabethan system and, by implication, against the queen
herself. That assault became known as the Essex revolt.

What, in fact, Essex was trying to do was to seize the
whole monopoly of power which the queen had hitherto shared among her ministers. It was nothing less than
an attempt to shift the pivot of authority from an old
queen to a young courtier. And around him there had
gathered a considerable body of angry young men : the
politically second-rate, the bankrupt, the disappointed,
as well as a section of the literary coterie of late Elizabethan London.

Essex had also another part to play; and here he did
the unforgivable thing. By his recalcitrance and insu-
bordination he openly assailed the total Elizabethan
myth, now more than forty years old. In a letter to
Lord Keeper Egerton he had not minced his words.
'What!' he asked, 'Cannot princes err? . . . Is an

earthly power or authority infinite? Pardon me! Pardon me! my good Lord. I can never subscribe to these principles!' According to Sir Walter Ralegh, he had once said to the queen that 'her conditions were as crooked as her carcase'. Here indeed was more than an attack on the Elizabethan system. In his own angry, clumsy way, he tried to tear down the whole apparatus of the Elizabethan cult. He tried to show that the virgin goddess was no more than a frail woman. It was the peculiar role of Essex to play the small boy who announced to the world the precise nature of the Emperor's new clothes.

This was Elizabeth's moment of truth. But it was not the last she would experience. 'It is credibly reported,' John Clapham, Burghley's secretary, tells us, 'that, not long before her death, she had a great apprehension of her own age and declination by seeing her face, then lean and full of wrinkles, truly represented to her in a glass.' She stared at the mirror for a long time, whereupon it began to dawn on her 'how often she had been abused by flatterers whom she held in too great estimation, that had informed her the contrary'.

Meanwhile Essex, the man who had once risen so high in stature, was now at the head of a hostile movement whose measure had not yet been taken. England was within sight of civil war. If that is clear enough to the historian, was it equally clear to the queen's greatest contemporary, William Shakespeare, who included in his play, *King John*, written in the period before the revolt, what seems no less than an appeal to Englishmen to heal their feuds and close their ranks, lest the nation should fall victim to Spanish power?—

> *This England never did—nor never shall—*
> *Lie at the proud foot of a conqueror,*
> *But when it first did help to wound itself.*

An incipient civil war was extinguished by the swift action of the queen and her ministers; and, on February 25, 1601, Essex was executed.

From whichever political angle we consider Essex, we must, I think, acknowledge that the queen's decision to finish with him, and in the end to execute him, rested on a sound analysis of the situation. It is only when we move out of politics into the human tragedy of these declining years that the Essex episode moves also into another sphere.

Essex was politically immature and, in his folly, placed himself in an impossible situation from which not even the queen could extricate him. It has sometimes been suggested that the adroit Cecil, once he foresaw the outcome of his rival's antics, gently manoeuvred him down the slope to his own destruction. But this remains sheer speculation. It may be that, when the materials for Cecil's and Essex's careers have been thoroughly explored, new light will fall on the detailed processes of these tragic months. But it is unlikely to call for any fundamental re-casting of their roles in history : the one, knight-errant, gallant, wayward and—in the world of politics—an amateur; the other, the devoted and patient administrator, bred from childhood for the exacting tasks of politics, old before he was young, with the long head of a statesman set upon the frail and twisted body of a boy.

Quem Deus vult perdere . . . ? It was madness for Essex to go to Ireland when he did, with all the odds piling up against him over there, while he left behind in London a body of hostile ministers. It was madness —and he knew it—to go on 'such an errand at such a time with so little comfort or ability from the Court of England to effect that I go about'. 'I spake,' he said, 'a language that was not understood or to a goddess not at leisure to hear prayers.'

But he was manifestly ill-equipped for the war of attrition in Ireland, or the squalid battles of intrigue at home, part of that other unyielding war of attrition which, in the end, saps men's souls and judgements. To him the council atmosphere in London, while his promotion and whole career were under discussion behind his back, was claustrophobic. He had looked often enough across the table into the ambiguous eyes of faction and could hardly breathe. He had to get out into the fresh air. As in the case of Mary, Queen of Scots, there is something inevitable in the tragedy of Essex.

His revolt was the first big attack on the Elizabethan system, against which it broke in vain. The second attack, coming in the same year, was more severe. It came from the last parliament of the reign. The government was by now perilously short of funds to meet its heavy commitments, and for that reason Parliament had been summoned. But for some time the crown had been using various unpopular methods for raising money, of which the most notorious was the sale of monopolies. By means of it, whole sectors of the economy had passed under the control of private monopolists who, by movements of the price level, could virtually hold the consumer to ransom. Resentment had been growing for years and, in 1597, in response to parliamentary protest, the queen had promised reform. Nothing had been done; and, in 1601, the exasperated Commons were preparing to take matters into their hands.

Here was a situation the queen hated most : a head-on constitutional collision. Alarmed by it, her ministers and others urged members to proceed by petition. Opposing them, many members wanted to proceed by bill. This was no mere dispute over formalities. In moving by bill the Commons were openly seizing the initiative and claiming a far greater share in government than any Tudor monarch had hitherto allowed. It was an attack on the queen's prerogative and as such she recognized it.

When Sir Francis Bacon—more prudent now than in 1593—defended the prerogative, his arguments were opposed by other members. When Sir Walter Ralegh attempted a defence of the royal policy, he was heard in hostile silence. When a Mr. Heyle was so unwise as to say that all men's property belonged to the queen, he was shouted down. In a deepening crisis, the queen at last recognized how profoundly her subjects were moved. Now she acted promptly against monopolies—virtually ceded total victory to the opposition—and parliamentary proceedings on this issue came to an end. Her prerogative, in theory, was still intact. But it had been a near thing; and Sir Robert Cecil betrayed the manifest embarrassment of the government when, on the eve of the Commons' victory, he told them that their behaviour was more fit for a grammar school than a Parliament.

We must of course be on our guard against exaggerating the importance of this parliamentary clash. By contrast, in religious matters—at least in Parliament—the queen and her subjects enjoyed a much greater harmony. The spectacular resistance of the Protestant activists had spent itself : Martin Marprelate seems to have had less effect upon his enemies than upon his friends. They drew back somewhat as they glimpsed whither the extremists were leading them. For the last years of the queen they seem to have preferred political discretion to pious valour. Hence the surprising calm with which the queen and her Parliament transacted so much of their business. But the economic problem was intractable : at least within the framework of Elizabethan government as then constructed; and the immediate effect of the monopolies debate must have been shattering. After that, it fell to the peculiar genius of the early Stuarts to intensify the economic hostility while they re-awakened the religious distrust until, with combined force, they swept Charles I from his throne.

The queen took the lesson gravely to heart and made one last attempt to set her house in order. She was indeed deeply troubled to see her own passion for economy swamped by an official lust for perquisites and extravagance, even in her own household. A faulty system encouraged it. In those days a good deal of the household provisions was obtained by purveyance, an antiquated procedure under which supplies were bought up well below the market price, only to be swallowed up by the unassuageable appetites of her armies of officials. Here was the promise of another scandal and she was resolved to stop it if she could. In the very last year of her reign she summoned Richard Brown, her clerk comptroller, and demanded of him an analytical comparison of household expenditure for the third and forty-third years of her reign. This was in due course provided; and it confirmed all the worst fears of the queen. The wretched Brown at once felt the full force of the royal displeasure:

> And shall I suffer this? Did I not tell you, Brown, what you would find? . . . I will not suffer this dishonourable spoil and increase that no prince ever before me did to the offence of God and the great grievance of my loving subjects . . . And now, myself understanding of it, they may justly accuse me to suffer it . . . But my speedy order for reformation shall satisfy my loving subjects grieved. For I will end as I began with my subjects' love . . .

No wonder, she said, there was parliamentary criticism; and she forthwith gave order for reform. But here

Brown had the last word. At the end of his account of these proceedings we have his brief, sanctimonious sigh of relief : 'In the meantime, before the fecting ([completion] whereof, it pleased God to take Her Majesty to His mercy.'

Until almost the end, the queen was still active. But it is hard to escape the feeling that, after the crises of 1601, she emerged with her spirit weakened and her prestige damaged. She had just over a year of life left to her : a clouded one in which she carried the memory of political faction and personal tragedy. She appears to have felt that the time had come to go.

She had been in reasonably good health all her life; and she seems to have suffered at the last from no easily identifiable disease. But in February 1603, while at Richmond, her energy and spirit gradually deserted her. She refused medicine and would not even take to her bed. Her ministers, including her young Secretary of State, Robert Cecil, her lord keeper, Egerton, her old archbishop, Whitgift, gathered round her. Her physicians apparently believed that her tough frame would last for many years yet; but the queen herself would have none of it. When the archbishop told her of her good prospects of recovery, she refused to listen. When he spoke of the joys of heaven, she eagerly grasped his hand. And finally, when her advisers recognized that she had given up the physical struggle and told her to prepare her soul for God, she calmly answered : 'That I have done long ago.'

'Remember, madam, that you are a mortal creature,'

her archbishop, Grindal, had told her as far back as 1576. 'You are a mighty prince,' he went on, 'yet remember that He which dwelleth in Heaven is mightier.' She had outlasted Grindal by two decades; but now the Supreme Governor of the church must prepare to render account to her overlord.

For the last day or two of her life she seems to have lost her powers of speech; but her understanding was good to the end. And then, in the early hours of March 24, 1603, her indomitable spirit, for the first time in her life, acknowledged defeat. At ten o'clock Sir Robert Cecil, accompanied by the great ministers of state, went down to the gates of Whitehall and proclaimed that James VI, King of Scots, had at last succeeded to his long-awaited inheritance.

Chapter Twelve

Elizabeth 1 and the English Nation

THE greatness of the Elizabethan age has frequently been identified with the personality of Elizabeth Tudor. That is how contemporaries saw it; and we who work, four centuries afterwards, on the surviving materials of the reign are inclined—perhaps too often —to see it in the same way. For she was the last English monarch whose name and fame were, from the start, intimately interwoven with the fabric of the English nation.

With her successors, the Stuarts, it was different. The bond wore thin and finally snapped. We can easily distinguish what seventeenth-century Englishmen achieved without help from the Stuarts—and, indeed, sometimes in spite of them. But, until they came, the destiny of monarch and nation seemed indissolubly linked. Especially was this true during the first half of Elizabeth's reign. Perhaps even until the Armada, a major blunder on her part might have shattered beyond repair the society and prospects of the young and inexperienced people committed to her care.

For these reasons the personality of the queen was a dominant theme in the prodigious volume of poetry—some of it of lyrical splendour, some sheer doggerel—which the times inspired. But it remains true, especially in the work of the playwrights and the propagandists, that we cannot always differentiate their faith in the nation from their adoration of the queen. If we may borrow a phrase from a poet of a much later age, it was the 'glad, confident morning' of English literature. There was a vigour, directness and flexibility of speech and writing, fully expressive of a young and virile nation. Sometimes the literature carried also an elegant complexity, associated most with John Lyly's *Euphues*, but displayed over a much wider field, including some of the queen's speeches. Here one recognizes the reflection in culture of the stilted splendours of that political masquerade which made up Elizabethan court life.

Nor did all the literature consist simply of paeans in praise of the Elizabethan government and order. The political speeches, the puritan pamphlets, at their best, had a frank and vivid candour which carried their barbed eloquence straight to their mark. And the greatest of the queen's subjects, Spenser, Ralegh, Shakespeare himself, included in their works mordant passages of political and social criticism.

In literature, Elizabethans won a European primacy. In music, too, Englishmen showed their native genius. Outstanding in an impressive list of composers was William Byrd, who gave new life to the sacred music of tradition. (Like a number of contemporary composers he combined faith in the old communion with a powerful contribution to the culture of Protestant England.) More insular perhaps—although it had its European roots—was the madrigal, whose sweet English joys, in the work of Thomas Morley and others, convey as nothing else can the domestic pleasures of a prospering middle class.

In the other arts there was rather less to show. There were fine portraits by men like Nicholas Hilliard and George Gower, but no one within measuring distance of the great foreign painters who had come to England, like Holbein in the early part of the century or Gheeraerts at the end. Indeed, some of the best minds in the arts and crafts of the Continent were attracted here by royal and aristocratic patronage. With their help, and a considerable body of English provincial talent, the aristocracy and gentry built sturdily and well : sometimes too well, to be overtaken by bankruptcy before the work was complete. But the veritable palaces like Burghley and Longleat, as well as the fine half-timbered manor houses scattered throughout the shires, remind us that they built to last. For the owners, their architects and craftsmen, it was also the glad, confident morning.

It was this same spirit which carried English ships and men, in exploration, trade—and sometimes plain piracy—beyond the limits of personal security and political prudence. Their importance lay, not so much in their performance, which could be acutely variable, but in their promise, and in the lessons that their unrewarding exploits often had to teach. It was a time, also, of England's imperial apprenticeship, when the first notions of colonization were evolved, by Hakluyt the younger and, most of all, in the seminal mind of Ralegh. In everything that Ralegh did in this sphere, he failed. But in his notions of overseas settlement and in his humane dealings with the natives—based, so he said, on direct instructions from the queen—he pointed to a concept which has re-emerged time and time again during the confused centuries of English imperialism.

What in fact did Elizabeth and her government achieve? In economic affairs they accomplished much less than they desired. Burghley himself spent un-measured hours brooding over reports, memoranda, statistical accounts, in search of a policy and the machinery to carry it out. A policy—or rather a loosely held group of policies—he found; and it was based on a stable, conservative society firmly planted in the soil. But these things were more easily proclaimed than established—or re-established.

Agriculture, he believed, was the framework of the English economy. If a choice had to be made between it and, for example, the textile industry, agriculture must override all. In the same way he believed that it was more important to grow corn than raise sheep. When his son, Robert Cecil, long afterwards said: 'Whosoever doth not maintain the plough destroys this kingdom,' he was speaking with his father's—and his monarch's—voice. In this, at least, time upheld his judgement. There were, of course, exceptions; but, in the main, where corn had grown before, corn grew again. Of course, men continued to move out of the country into the towns, but a good many textile workers went the other way, in search of water power—as well as freedom from urban gild restraints. For centuries, until indeed about a hundred years ago, there were more Englishmen living in the country than in the towns. But it was economic forces, not the high endeavours of ministers, which held the nation to its agrarian roots.

For a time, until the middle of the sixteenth century, it had looked to some people as though the whole face of England would be changed by the intruding sheep. The wool gave a better harvest than corn, for the overseas demand for cloth was heavy, and made heavier by the depreciated pound. But conversion to sheep-runs had led to some eviction of the peasantry as their cornlands went down under pasture and their cottages went the way of their corn. There had been some social dislocation, too, rich fuel for the inflammatory speeches of the moralists. But in the early fifties the inflated market began, for various reasons, to shrink; while the currency purification, carried through by Elizabeth in 1561, helped to bring some degree of general stability. The economic scales began to tip back towards corn and against wool, under pressure of changing prices and markets, more effective than government exhortation and enactment. For the greater part of Elizabeth's reign the agricultural scene, although changing here and there, was relatively firm in its established contours.

In industry, more particularly strategic industry, government intervention had rather more to show for its pains. Dominated as it was by the threat of war, the crown made heroic efforts to erect an armaments industry in England, and thereby break its risky dependence on overseas supplies. The raw materials of war, copper and zinc ores for the brass cannon of the day, were the especial targets of its anxious search. Foreign skill and capital were offered attractive terms; the queen's own money, and that of her courtiers, was poured into the enterprise. At first the results were bitterly disappointing : the fruits of technical difficulties, financial scarcity, labour troubles. But by the end of the century there was even a stimulating overseas demand for English cannon, already held in high esteem : the first dim shadows of the great coming events in English industrial history.

Coal, too, was casting its long shadow before it. For centuries, the few Englishmen who lived near the material had scratched at the surface of the earth for handfuls. But it was not until the second half of the sixteenth century that the exploitation of some of these mineral resources was seriously begun. In the Newcastle district especially, there developed a flourishing coal industry—as well as an obstinate monopoly of merchants who made the London consumers go red in the face. Industry would have far to go before it could understand and adjust itself to this powerful and mysterious material. But, in the domestic fireplaces, the transfer from timber to coal was easily and eagerly accomplished, provided that transport—mostly by water—could carry the coal. To the Elizabethans it was one more sign of their rising standard of living.

'When we sit in our lodging,' wrote Robert Cecil from
Ostend to his father, 'we look all as pale and wan as
ashes by the smoke of our turfs, which makes me envy
Your Lordship's porter that sits all day by a sweet fire
of sea-coal in your lodge.'

Sometimes the pace of industry quickened, but its
basic shape remained unaltered. Historians today see
little during the period of that industrial revolution
which excited some of their predecessors twenty-five
years ago. Over the greater part of the country the
main source of fuel was not coal but timber, as it had
been for centuries; the main instrument of power was
not machinery but the human muscle, allied where
practicable with water power. In most places tradition held fast.

But, under pressure of trade difficulties, Englishmen
were exploring new materials and new markets. The
heavy English woollen cloth, which had warmed the
backs of Europe for centuries, had less to recommend
it farther south in the Mediterranean lands and beyond. The new, lighter textiles—cheaper to produce,
easier to fabricate—diversified the English textile industry and gave it a place in the sun.

All this took place amid the great debate of the
period as to whether trade should be free for all, with
each merchant finding his own way to the centre of
demand and negotiating his own price; or whether
the Merchant Adventurers, a corporation of rich and
powerful traders, should dominate the field, lay down

the conditions of commerce and portion it out according to their beliefs and tastes.

In this, the queen's government held no doctrinaire views, although it preferred stability and control to wild speculation. So, in a sense, did the Merchant Adventurers, provided that they exercised the control. With the power of a well-filled purse, they accordingly put heavy pressure on the government, sometimes with success, to obtain an overwhelming share of the trade, old and new. In the process, they looked on Parliament with different eyes from those of, say, Peter Wentworth—or those of the constitutional historian.

The Merchant Adventurers were not concerned, as Wentworth was, with the House of Commons as the crucible of English liberties. To them it was a pressure centre upon the economic policies of the government: to gain special measures here, neutralize hostile legislation there. All too often a well-conceived bill might be emasculated in Parliament by the Merchant Adventurers lobby or some other group; or exemptions and licences sold by a government sadly short of cash. However worthy its aims, it lacked the financial independence to pursue a wholly national policy. 'Merchants have grown so cunning in the trade of corrupting', runs a memorandum, 'and found it so sweet, that since the [first year of] Henry VIII there could never be won any good law or order which touched their liberty or state, but they stayed it, either in the Commons, or higher House of Parliament, or else by the prince himself.' The

memorandum is dated 1559: it would have served
equally well for 1599.

Here was the crux of the matter. However well conceived the plans of the queen and her ministers, she
lacked the economic staying power to hold fast to her
policies, if any notable opposition emerged. That is the
other side of the constitutional coin. In religion and
foreign policy she did fight hard, with a considerable
measure of success. In economic matters it was more
difficult. All too often the merchants refused to pay
the government piper until they had called their com-
mercial tune.

In general, the queen was skilful in handling the parliamentary machine. And she could make bold assertions of her high prerogative. But at the end, in the
changing realities of the situation, her claims carried
less and less conviction. Her forceful and moving affirmations of her ancient rights sound sometimes as
though she were whistling to keep her courage up in
the dark. This is not to say that, given greater room to
manoeuvre, either she or Burghley would have wanted
to pursue some adventurous or revolutionary line.
Quite the reverse. She never lost her vision of a stable,
paternalist society in which each man knew his 'degree',
his secure station in life, and kept to it. But it was
easier said than done.

The very emphasis upon 'degree' which one meets
in literature and politics is a sign of anxiety about a
system which is passing away. Elizabeth herself believed that the churchmen, the nobility and the com-

mons each had their appointed rank in the social order;
and she preferred them to know their place. She was
sparing in the grant of honours. Few of her ministers
were raised to the House of Lords; there was a continuous flow in that direction under the more expansive
James I. James was prodigal in money and honours;
she in neither. She favoured a backward looking,
ordered social hierarchy. But she could not arrest the
forces of social change.

In many ways the nation was fluid. But the leaders
of society—including those who had just arrived—preferred a more formalized system, with rank clearly
marked and, it was hoped, permanent. All this, according to a famous Shakespearean passage, reflected the
ordered harmony of the universe. If the nation did not
sustain this ordered pattern of rank, continued Shakespeare's Ulysses, the whole system would flounder into
anarchy :

> *Force should be right; or rather, right and wrong . . .*
> *Should lose their names, and so should justice, too.*
> *Then everything includes itself in power,*
> *Power into will, will into appetite.*

Perhaps the queen's greatest poet, like her greatest
minister—and herself—was something of a conservative.

The profound uneasiness in face of change is manifest in the lines we have just quoted, and in so much
else in Elizabethan literature and legislation. The
Statute of Apprentices of 1563, for example, tried to
contain whole sectors of the English economy within

a medieval framework, at a time when the textile industry, in its unruly developments, was threatening to
burst at the seams. The poor law policy tried to keep
unemployment and poverty within its local bounds, to
be relieved by local charity : it was the same policy of
social containment.

Much of Tudor social policy was indeed cruel and
inhuman. A homeless vagabond, guilty of no particular crime, could be sentenced to be whipped until
his, or her, 'back shall be bloody'. Whipping was the
punishment also, for the parents of illegitimate
children. A child could itself be separated from its
mother and sent back to the parish of its birth, since
with that parish rested ultimate responsibility for poor
relief. 'The woman Elner Clerke', decreed the Wilt-
shire justices of the peace in 1582, 'is to remain in the
sheriff's custody, and the child is to be carried from
tithing to tithing until it comes to the place where it
was born, namely at Melksham.'

The severity of some of these measures was one more
sign of the weakness of government, in this case locally,
as well as a reflection of the deep social anxiety of the
age. The countryside was, from time to time, made
noisy with the tramp of the sturdy beggar, a modest
name for the thieves and murderers who held all life
cheap, including their own. But to its credit, when the
negative policy of repression was found faulty, the
government, local and then central, evolved a new conception, crowned by the consolidating statutes of 1598.

Under the legislation of that year, the financing of

social welfare, developed during the last half century, was confirmed; and the chain of social responsibility, right through from the most remote parish to the Privy Council in London, was made emphatic and coherent —at least in theory. At the same time, the savage penalties for vagrancy were alleviated: an acknow-ledgement that unemployment and poverty were not necessarily the results of personal defects in character. It was a sign also that the problem was being brought under control.

Here, too, the Elizabethans built to last. These main outlines of welfare policy served the nation on into the nineteenth century, until Englishmen forgot the lessons which their Elizabethan ancestors had learned; and they began to dismantle the whole system.

Other elements in the Elizabethan state possessed less powers of survival. For this the explanation lies in part in the Elizabethan system itself. It possessed many of the attributes of personal monarchy and displayed many of the trappings of power. But the instruments of government were primitive; and money—the sinews of government as of war—had to be stretched beyond its limits.

Locally the queen relied upon her lord lieutenant as the senior military authority in his shire or shires. Some-times he served her to the best of his ability although, quite often, that did not add up to much. In any case he was usually an unpaid landed aristocrat who had no great urge or capacity to turn his badly trained, in-voluntary levies into an effective fighting force. Any thorough investigation into the system of recruiting and training usually brought to light plenty of unsavoury scandals but not much to encourage any warlike zeal in the government.

For local administration there were the meetings of the justices of the peace at quarter sessions: an assembly of amateurs coming together for two or three days every three months to deal with civil as well as criminal affairs. They often did their best, under instruction from the Privy Council and, at times, from the High Court judges coming on assize. But their best, also, did not amount to much; and, to carry out policy —even if they wanted to—they could raise very little in the way of funds and no more in the way of service, from the defective parish officials pressed, on occasion, into their unwelcome duties. Here, as in so much else, practice lagged reluctantly behind theory.

In maintaining law and order however the justices of the peace played a not insignificant part. To reinforce them there were the assize judges, the common law courts in Westminster, and the prerogative courts like Star Chamber. These again did much; but they too had but a tenuous hold upon the shires. A quarrel between neighbours over some disputed acre of land could lead, it is true, to a whole series of lawsuits extending into the most likely—and unlikely—of courts. But it would often be accompanied by any number of bloody scuffles between the followers of the disputants. English society at this stage, by a paradox, was both litigious and lawless.

Whether Englishmen were in fact free in Elizabethan society—whether indeed there was a Tudor
despotism—has led to vigorous controversy spreading over the intervening centuries. Certainly one
remains impressed by the wide range of the government's intentions and instructions. But no less impressive is the large section of public life upon which the
government's grasp was feeble, intermittent and in-
secure. Distance imposed handicaps; so did the bad
system of communications; so did the pervasive shortage of royal officials and royal revenues. So did down-
right sabotage of policy in the shires. In the light of all
this, what is remarkable is not the failures of the central
administration but its relative degree of success.

Corruption, too, there was; and some of it reached
high into the queen's councils and administration. But
that, also, derived in part from the perilous scarcity of
royal revenues. The queen could never pay her ministers and officials the full rewards for the services they
rendered. Whether she liked it or not, she had to leave
them to obtain what they could in the unofficial gifts
from the public at large. Even the highest officers of
state, in the performance of their public duties, received
gifts. The same was true of their servants, and of their
servants' servants. (For this was a time not only of currency inflation but of departmental inflation also, right
through the government service, central and local.)
Here was a crude and decadent method of public
finance : a haphazard system of indirect taxation. But
it was not always corrupt; it attracted able men; and
it enabled the queen's government to go on. In the

absence of sufficient governmental revenue there was no other way.

Elizabethan administration, both central and local, was in many respects a rickety affair. The queen never succeeded in extracting from her subjects an adequate contribution to the cost of government; nor did she always succeed in imposing unpopular policies upon the politically significant part of the nation. All this she knew. If she did not do all the things some of her vigorous subjects thought she should, at home or abroad, it may be, as some believed, because she lacked the desire to do so. But no less important, she lacked the power, the money and the machinery.

Above all, by the end of the reign, Elizabeth had reached a stage in her relations with Parliament when the increasingly urgent constitutional problems were insoluble within the existing framework of society. Through their control of direct taxation, the parliamentary classes made a bid for greater legislative power. Their wealth, relative to that of the queen, had sharply increased. They had also some pungent views on the political, religious, economic and diplomatic issues of the day, in which they felt that their interests were as much involved as were those of the monarchy. But still she held them, with dwindling success, to the guiding reins on which her grandfather had held their grandfathers. They tugged hard at them; they tried sometimes to run before they could walk. On occasion it looked as though neither they nor the queen would get anywhere. And at such times they were particularly reluctant to grant her the taxation she so desperately needed. They forced upon Queen Elizabeth a hand-to-mouth existence. And upon the early Stuarts they forced outright deadlock.

Nearly a century would pass after her death before the monarch would again find a *modus vivendi* with Parliament. And that solution would be found only after rebellion, two civil wars and another rebellion. It would be found, also, at the expense of the monarchy.

To these complexities which faced the queen was added a further one, whose outlines are only now being discovered—and disputed over—by historians. This involves the whole structure of provincial England. For the English countryside, never entirely stable, was in many places changing its whole social balance. The traditional relationships would take a long time to dissolve; but the impact of new ideas and new attitudes was sharply felt in the century which followed the English Reformation.

A class, or part of a class—very loosely called the gentry—was able in some cases to gain an economic ascendancy, as compared with the aristocracy above them and the yeomanry and peasantry below. Not all the gentry rose in wealth and influence; not all of those who did rise did so for the same reasons. Some knew better than their neighbours how to exploit the land; others knew better how to exploit the opportunities of office. Others failed miserably in both. If some of the causes of this upward and downward movement are still speculative, what is less in doubt is that the countryside—and the crown—were alike feeling the impact of a thrusting gentry. In the country it showed itself here and there in the gathering pace of agricultural change. In the capital, when Parliament met, it displayed its eager challenge for political power.

If the queen hesitated to press any issue too far, it was because she considered that her task was a holding task : to preserve the system as she had inherited it, to leave the solution of its problems to a later day. This is the key to any understanding of her age, particularly in its later decades. As a conception of government, it may lack creative force or heroic inspiration. But for long it was sound, practical politics.

For there *was* a theme in Elizabeth's life and reign, and that was the unremitting search to bind the nation in unity after two decades of discord in the time of her father, brother and sister. These views she held with passion, often in the teeth of opposition from minister and Parliament alike. This principle gave meaning to her religious policy, her social policy, her relations with Parliament. Within its broad limits she gave herself plenty of room to move, but the dominant necessity of the age was never far from her mind. That is what she meant, after the greatest political storm of her reign—the monopolies debate of 1601—when she said : 'Though God hath raised me high, yet this I account the glory of my crown, that I have reigned with your loves.' In these words also, so near to the close of her life, she answered the early wooing of the unknown poet whom we quoted at the end of our first chapter.

In religion, above all, she succeeded for her time. By the end of her reign, the fierce tempests of the earlier years had died down. Neither Puritanism nor Catholicism were broken forces : but both were leaderless and divided. Puritanism would re-emerge, first in moderation, then in extremism, in the half century after the queen's death. Catholicism, in the late nineties, had been going through a good deal of heart-searching, focused upon the so-called archpriest controversy, as to whether good Catholics must pursue a policy made and led from abroad, or should seek to become a loyal and tolerated minority in a Protestant state. The extremist fringe had their day in the Gunpowder Plot of 1605, the last flicker of a discredited campaign. The majority of Catholics found a way of life in due time which embraced Catholic idealism as well as political conformity. In this, at least, the queen's hopes were—long after her day—fulfilled. The measure of unity, achieved under Elizabeth, was lost under the early Stuarts. But it came again.

Elizabeth, it is true, believed that the unity she valued above all things must be focused upon the divinity of the monarchy; and, in time, she came to delight too much in its attributes, and to exploit them for reasons other than those of state. But, if we look back over her reign, these human failings seem small compared with those which afflicted monarchy before and after her day.

Failure and tragedy at the end cannot for long obscure the greatness of the Elizabethan achievement. For the weaknesses which had emerged are inherent in any system of personal monarchy if it lasts on into an age of transition to a new governmental order. Yet, to measure what Elizabeth accomplished we need only look back for a moment to the opening of her reign.

The twenty-five years which elapsed between the birth of Elizabeth and her accession to the throne were the most momentous in the sixteenth century and are, indeed, without parallel in modern English history, with the possible exception of the twenty-five years ending at the Congress of Vienna in 1815, or the twenty-five years through which the present generation has just been living. During the first twenty-five years of Elizabeth's lifetime, England underwent more changes in religion than she or any other nation in Europe has undergone in the four centuries which have since elapsed. During those twenty-five years, also, England experienced a wave of inflation of dimensions and social consequences unsurpassed until the twentieth century. During those twenty-five years England hovered uncertainly between two destinies : that of remaining a small, divided, second-class power or of laying the foundations of her imperial greatness. This question was unresolved when Elizabeth came to the throne in 1558. By the time that she died it had been answered.

In north-western Europe, in the second half of the sixteenth century, there were four women who governed their countries. Three of them, Mary Tudor, Mary, Queen of Scots and Catharine de Medici of

France, left their countries worse than they found them. Each fulfilled the savage prophecy of John Knox about the monstrous regiment of women. The fourth woman ruler, Elizabeth Tudor, was the exception. England, in 1603, was still burdened with constitutional problems unresolved, and economic and diplomatic issues still uncertain. But it passed on to James I as a secure and united heritage. This single-minded passion for unity—and its fulfilment—gives Elizabeth her secure place in the history of English statesmanship.

'Here now will I rest my troubled mind', wrote Sir John Harrington, Queen Elizabeth's godson, as he retired to the country after her death, 'and tend my sheep like an Arcadian swain that hath lost his fair mistress. For in sooth I have lost the best and fairest love that ever shepherd knew, even my gracious queen. And sith my good mistress is gone, I shall not hastily put forth for a new master.' He had served the queen with duty and affection ; and we owe to him some of the wisest opinions of her during her later life. But now, having basked with the best of men in the warm sunshine of the queen, he had no pleasure in contemplating the colder wind blowing down from the north. For he knew that the old order was closing ; and he had doubts of what would come with the opening of the new.

Note on Further Reading

The best life of Queen Elizabeth is by Sir John Neale (1934); while his magistral volumes, *The Elizabethan House of Commons* (1949) and *Elizabeth I and Her Parliaments* (1953, 1957) are indispensable for a scholarly understanding of the constitution. Conyers Read's biography of William Cecil (1956, 1960) is more than a study of the queen's leading minister and is invaluable for the politics and diplomacy of the age.

The best general accounts of the Tudor period are :

S. T. BINDOFF, *Tudor England* (1950) and
G. R. ELTON, *England under the Tudors* (1955).

J. B. BLACK's *The Reign of Elizabeth* (2nd ed., 1959) is thorough and scholarly, with an excellent bibliography.

A. L. ROWSE's *The England of Elizabeth* (1950) is a valuable survey of many aspects of Elizabethan society; and E. P. CHEYNEY's *History of England from the Defeat of the Armada to the Death of Elizabeth* (1914, 1926) is especially useful on government and administration. For the Tudor period as a whole, the best source is G. R. ELTON, *The Tudor Constitution* (1960). A. G. R. SMITH's *The Government of Elizabethan England* (1967) is a good brief introduction.

For ecclesiastical developments there are :

W. H. FRERE, *The English Church in the reigns of Elizabeth and James I* (1904).

P. COLLINSON, *The Elizabethan Puritan Movement* (1967).

P. MCGRATH, *Puritans and Papists under Elizabeth I* (1967).

For naval and imperial aspects especially helpful are:

J. A. WILLIAMSON, *The Age of Drake* (1938).

A. L. ROWSE, *The Expansion of Elizabethan England* (1955).

D. B. QUINN, *Raleigh and the British Empire* (1947).

G. MATTINGLY, *The Defeat of the Spanish Armada* (1959).

For the army there are: C. G. CRUIKSHANK, *Elizabeth's Army* (2nd ed., 1966), and L. BOYNTON, *The Elizabethan Militia, 1558-1638* (1967).

The best short account of economic developments is in P. RAMSEY, *Tudor Economic Problems* (1963), while for agrarian developments, *The Agrarian History of England and Wales*, vol. iv, 1500-1640, ed. JOAN THIRSK (1967) is invaluable. G. UNWIN's *Studies in Economic History* (1926) and W. R. SCOTT's *Joint Stock Companies* (1910-12) remain important. L. STONE's *The Crisis of the Aristocracy 1558-1641* (1965; abridged edition, 1967) is an illuminating piece of social analysis; but the controversy over the gentry can only be followed in successive issues of the *Economic History Review*.

For the thought of the period, J. W. ALLEN's *History of Political Thought in the Sixteenth Century* (1928) remains the standard work, which should be accompanied with C. MORRIS's stimulating *Political Thought in England from Tyndale to Hooker* (1953) and E. M. W. TILLYARD's *The Elizabethan World Picture* (1943). *Shakespeare's England* (1917) contains some excellent essays and illustrations.

C. READ's *Bibliography of English History, Tudor Period* (2nd ed., 1959) is an exhaustive survey of the materials, as well as of the published work on the period.

Index